南京信息工程大学教材立项项目
南京信息工程大学国际教育学院暨孔子学院专项

校园微镜头：我的大学

主　编　刘金华　马航飞　吴鹏飞
副主编　鲁晶石　高　明　王曼蓉
　　　　龙周娜　韦杰卓

气象出版社
China Meteorological Press

内容简介

本书是一套专门针对汉语视听类课程设计的短视频赏析综合语言教材。教材内容丰富，形式生动，涉及文化选题广，视听素材选自当代的中国大学校园，主要围绕年轻人的校园日常生活展开，结合“视”“听”双重语言输入渠道，为学习者搭建基于自然语言的课堂教学环境，将汉语视听学习、讲练与了解当代中国现状有效融合于一体。本书练习题设计灵活，兼容了不同层次的汉语学习需要，可供海外中文爱好者、在校学生以及专业汉语学习者按需选用。

图书在版编目（CIP）数据

校园微镜头 ： 我的大学 ： 汉文、英文 / 刘金华, 马航飞，吴鹏飞主编. -- 北京 ： 气象出版社， 2024. 10. -- ISBN 978-7-5029-8328-4

Ⅰ. H195.4

中国国家版本馆 CIP 数据核字第 2024ZT2017 号

校园微镜头：我的大学

Xiaoyuan Weijingtou：Wo de Daxue

出版发行：气象出版社

地　　址：北京市海淀区中关村南大街 46 号　　邮政编码：100081

电　　话：010-68407112（总编室）　010-68408042（发行部）

网　　址：http://www.qxcbs.com　　E-mail：qxcbs@cma.gov.cn

责任编辑：黄红丽　毛红丹　　终　　审：张　斌

责任校对：张硕杰　　责任技编：赵相宁

封面设计：艺点设计

印　　刷：北京建宏印刷有限公司

开　　本：710 mm×1000 mm　1/16　　印　　张：9.5

字　　数：190 千字

版　　次：2024 年 10 月第 1 版　　印　　次：2024 年 10 月第 1 次印刷

定　　价：70.00 元

编委会

特别致谢：

刘丰果　张　峰　邓博文　丁鹏飞　刘婉如　刘可夫
罗羽涵　玛　雅　米小芾　王奕鸥　伍　粤　魏一荣
徐雅杰　薛敬予　张文杉　陈泽华　高　鑫　拉姆斯秋
李煜晨　秦艺芯　任　泰　张恒睿

---

① 吴鹏飞，男，博士，南京信息工程大学遥感与测绘工程学院，助理研究员；
② 吴鹏飞，男，南京信息工程大学文学院，2023 届本科毕业生，现东南大学硕士研究生。

PREFACE 前言

21 世纪以来，高等教育国际化作为世界高等教育发展的重要趋势，被各国置于教育政策的核心位置，学生的国际流动成为高等教育国际化的显著特征。在这种情况下，尤其共建“一带一路”十年间，伴随着“汉语热”在全球范围的兴起，我国已成为亚洲最大留学目的国。本教学团队在前期对本校留学生汉语教学实践的基础上，以后疫情时代汉语学习为目标，将在华留学生汉语教学与当代中国高校文化高度融合，策划设计了《校园微镜头：我的大学》汉语视听说教材。

《校园微镜头：我的大学》以南京信息工程大学（下简称南信大）为场景蓝本，在特定的场合与实际背景下激发学生适时恰当而又不失真实乐趣的对话交流，内容紧贴在校留学生的实际生活、本土环境与时代特色。同时，在继承听说法优势的基础上，有效结合交际法、任务法、以学生为中心等新的方法和理念，克服了单纯使用听说法教学的弊端。以“实用、轻松、新颖”三大原则作为编撰此本教材的核心主旨，以“了解中国当代大学文化，培养综合运用语言的能力”为教学目标，以短小精悍、丰富有趣而又便于记忆的对话作为主要教学内容，对学生进行“听说领先，听说读写技能综合训练”，充分体现了以学生为中心、在互动中学习和启发式教学的新型汉语学习模式。

本教材紧贴当代留学生大学生活设计，视频方式灵活，题材新颖，涉及文化选题广，适用于汉语各阶段学习者。教师可以根据实际情况灵活使用本教材。比如在综合汉语课导入部分使用，以及用于听力、口语及文化专项讨论等。以上是对本教材使用方法的一些说明和建议，希望这本小书能够对汉语学习者提高听力水平、了解中国当代大学文化有所助益。

本书是南京信息工程大学教材立项项目，并得到南京信息工程大学国际教育学院暨孔子学院专项资助，特此鸣谢。教材所有短视频、文案及大部分照片均为南京信息工程大学师生原创。由于新冠疫情影响，教材从立项、制作到完成，中间经受很多波折。如今出版，最应该感谢的是这些年来一起参与的师生。少数图片、照片等资料及视频出镜由于时间、地域、联系渠道等多方面的限制，使用时未署姓名，还请版权人能够拨冗与我们联系，希望再版时能有机会一一修正。

编　者

2023 年 11 月 20 日

目 录 CONTENTS

第二单元　校园活动篇
Unit 2　Campus Activities

第三单元　校园生活篇
Unit 3　Campus Life

第一单元　校园介绍篇
Unit 1 Introduction to Campus

1 校园里的相遇
Encounters on campus

热身 WARMING UP

欢迎大家来到大学校园！在大学里，我们可以学习各种各样的知识，了解多姿多彩的文化，认识来自世界各地的朋友……初次见面，请向同学们介绍一下自己吧！

观看视频 WATCHING THE VIDEO

在大学校园里，一个中国学生和一个外国学生相遇了，他们会发生什么故事呢？

扫描视频二维码观看

内容提示 CONTENT TIPS

Part 1

课文 text

校园里的相遇

韦杰卓：我叫韦杰卓，我来南京信息工程大学（南信大）两年了，是汉语国际教育专业的学生。

米　雅：我叫米雅，我来南信大学习国际贸易，差不多三年了。

韦杰卓、米雅：我们的生活平平无奇，直到有一天我们在课堂上相遇。

韦杰卓：明天我们一起去拍照好吗？

米　雅：好的！

韦杰卓：我喜欢给她拍好看的照片，教她中文，介绍中国的文化。

米　雅：认识她以后，我吃到了很多中国美食，了解了很多中国文化，我越来越喜欢中国了。

韦杰卓、米雅：感谢南信大让我们相遇。

生词 new words

南信大 nánxìndà [n.]Abbreviation of Nanjing University of Information Science and Technology

汉语国际教育 hànyǔ guójì jiàoyù [n.] Teaching of Chinese as a Second Language

专业 zhuānyè [n.] major

国际贸易 guójì màoyì [n.]International Trade Major

差不多 chàbuduō [adv.] almost, nearly, just about

平平无奇 píngpíng-wúqí [adj.] ordinary, unattractive

相遇 xiāngyù [v.] meet

给 gěi [prep.] for

介绍 jièshào [v.] introduce

美食 měishí [n.] delicious food，delicacy

了解 liǎojiě [v.] understand

越来越 yuèláiyuè more and more

Part 2 注释 notes

1. 差不多

[副词] 表示“接近、几乎”的意思，可以用在动词、形容词、数量短语之前。例如：

[adv.] It means near or almost, which can be used before a verb, an adjective or a quantity phrase. For example:

① 我的作业差不多写完了。
② 他们两个人差不多一样高。
③ 这些东西差不多一百元。
④ 差不多八点了，快上课了。

2. 平平无奇

成语，指某事很普通，没有什么出色的地方，没有吸引人的地方。例如：

Idiom, referring to something is very common, there is nothing outstanding, there is no attraction. For example:

① 这篇文章平平无奇，不值得阅读。
② 他看起来平平无奇，居然是奥运冠军。

3. 我喜欢给她拍好看的照片，教她中文。

介词“给”可以用来引出动作、行为的接受对象。例如：

The preposition “给” may be used to introduce the recipient of an action or a behavior. For example:

① 昨天我给你打电话了。
② 妈妈给我做饭。

双宾句 The sentence with a ditransitive verb as its predicate.

汉语中某些动词（如“给、送、教、问”）可以带两个宾语，前一个是间接宾语（一般指人），后一个是直接宾语（一般指事物）。这种句子叫双宾句。例如：

Some verbs in Chinese may take two objects, the first being the indirect object (normally referring to persons) and the second being the direct object (normally referring to things). Such a sentence is known as the sentence with a ditransitive verb as its predicate. For example:

S①	V②	$O_1$③	O_2
我	给	他	一本书
妈妈	送	我	生日礼物
李老师	教	我们	中文
我	问	老师	问题

① S代表主语，下同；
② V代表谓语，下同；
③ O代表宾语，下同。

4. 我来南信大两年了。

语气助词“了”用于句尾，表示发生或完成。例如：

The modal particle “了” can be used at the end of a sentence, indicating occurrence or completion. For example:

① 他去吃饭了。

② 我写完作业了。

5. 我吃到了很多中国美食。

动态助词“了”用于动词后带宾语。动词后的宾语前面一般要有定语，如数量词或形容词、代词等。例如：

The aspect particle “了” can also be used between a verb and its object. There is usually a modifier before the object of the verb, such as a numeral classifier, an adjective or a pronoun, etc. For example:

S	V	了	O
我	买	了	一本书
老师	教	了	第一课
玛丽	去	了	图书馆

6. 我越来越喜欢中国了。

“越来越”的后边加上形容词或心理动词，如“越来越冷”“越来越喜欢”表示随着时间的推移，程度上发生的变化。注意，形容词或心理动词的前边都不能再加程度副词，不能说“越来越很热”“越来越非常想”。例如：

Followed by an adjective or a mental verb as in “越来越冷” (colder and colder) and “越来越喜欢” (like...more and more), “越来越” indicates the change in degree occurs as time passes by. Note that no adverb of degree is used before the adjective or mental verb, so phrases like “越来越很热” and “越来越非常想” are unacceptable. For example:

① 我认识的汉字越来越多了。

② 小丽越来越漂亮了。

语气助词“了”用在陈述句句尾，表示情况有了变化，或出现了新的情况，如“我现在没钱了”，表示“我”以前有钱，现在没有钱的变化。例如：

Used at the end of a declarative sentence, the modal particle “了” indicates a change in the situation or the occurrence of a new situation. For example, “我现在没钱了” means “I used to have money, but now I don't”, implying a change. For example:

① 昨天很冷，今天天气不那么冷了。
② 我现在喜欢运动了。
③ 我现在不喜欢夏天了。
④ 去年买的衣服今年不能穿了。

综合练习　COMPREHENSIVE PRACTICE

Part 1　视频练习

看视频，判断对错　Watch the video and judge true or false

1. 韦杰卓是汉语国际教育专业的学生。 (　　)
2. 米雅来中国已经三年了。 (　　)
3. 她们不是同班同学。 (　　)
4. 米雅喜欢给韦杰卓拍照片。 (　　)
5. 韦杰卓教米雅中文。 (　　)

看视频，选择填空　Watch the video and choose the best answer

1. 这是韦杰卓和米雅什么时候做的事？ (　　)

A．认识前　　B. 刚认识　　C. 认识后

2. 韦杰卓吃了什么？ (　　)

A．披萨　　B. 咖啡　　C. 面条

3. 他们是在哪里相遇的？ (　　)

A．图书馆　　B. 教室　　C. 操场

4. 韦杰卓在教米雅什么？　　　　（　　）

A．英语　　　　B. 中文　　　　C. 日语

看视频，回答问题　Watch the video and answer the questions

1. 为什么她们的生活平平无奇？
2. 米雅和韦杰卓认识后去做了什么？
3. 米雅为什么越来越喜欢中国了？

Part 2　书面练习

选词填空　Choose a word to fill in each blank

平平无奇　了解　相遇　美食　给

1. A：你们是怎么认识的？
   B：我们是在图书馆________的。
2. A：他看起来________，没想到居然是一个画家。
   B：是啊，他还是一个美术老师呢！
3. A：这是什么？
   B：这是朋友________我的礼物。
4. A：你怎么知道玛丽会迟到？
   B：因为我们是好朋友，我非常________她。
5. A：你为什么想去四川？
   B：因为四川的________很多。

完成句子　Complete the sentences

1. 我是____________________的学生。（专业）
2. 我来中国______________了。（差不多）
3. 我__________________运动。（越来越……）
4. 我们班来了一位新同学，__________________________。（介绍）

连词成句　Match the words into a sentence

1. 给　小王　我　水　一瓶

____

2. 他　画画　教　安娜

____

3. 一个　告诉　好消息　妈妈　我

____

4. 他　大家　叫　李老师

____

Part 3　拓展练习

角色扮演　Role-play

两人一组，一人扮演韦杰卓，一人扮演米雅。想象一下：当韦杰卓和米雅在课堂上相遇时，她们会聊些什么？

提示词：年龄、专业、爱好……

复述课文　Repeat the text

韦杰卓是……，她来……了。米雅来南信大……，差不多……。她们的生活……，直到有一天……。她们相遇后，会一起去……。韦杰卓喜欢……，教……，介绍……。认识韦杰卓以后，米雅吃到了……，了解了……，她越来越……。

小组活动　Group work

3~4 人一组，互相询问并记录小组成员和朋友在校园里的活动，每组请一位同学报告情况。例如：

A：你在校园里认识谁了？

B：我认识了迈克，他是电子信息专业的学生。

A：认识他以后，你们一起去做了什么？

B：我们一起去体育馆打了篮球。

记录表：

序号	朋友名字	专业	地点	做什么
1	迈克	电子信息	体育馆	打篮球

文化链接　CULTURAL LINK

1. 风筝　Kite

风筝在中国已有两千多年历史。传说哲学家墨子以前用三年时间制成一只木鸟，但只飞了一天就坏了，这便是中国历史上最早的风筝。风筝最初用来传递信息，而到了唐代和宋代的时候，放风筝已经成为人们所喜爱的一项户外娱乐活动。放风筝非常有趣，有益于身心健康。风筝作为中国的传统文化和民间艺术，在长期发展的过程中，产生出了许多种类、样式和流派（liúpài, 指文艺、学术等方面的派别），其中以北京、天津、山东潍坊、四川、广东所制的风筝最为著名。中国风筝图案将人物、花、鸟等形象与有独特意义的文字组合，创造了很多优秀的艺术品。

Kites have been used in China for over 2000 years. Legend has it that the philosopher Mozi used to make a wooden bird in three years, but it only flew for one day before it broke down, making it the earliest kite in Chinese history. Kites were first used to send messages, but by the Tang and Song Dynasties, kite flying had become a popular outdoor recreational activity. Kite flying was fun and good for the body and mind. As a traditional Chinese culture and folk art, kites have developed over a long period of time into many types, styles and schools (liú pài, literary and academic schools), of which the kites made in Beijing, Tianjin, Weifang in Shandong, Sichuan and Guangdong are the most famous. Chinese kite patterns combine images of people, flowers and birds with words of unique meaning, creating many excellent works of art.

2. 剪纸　Paper-cutting

剪纸是一门在中国民间流传近千年的工艺。对于熟练的剪纸艺人而言，这是一门即兴的艺术。他们没有稿纸，只需一把剪刀便可剪出无数种图案。而围绕剪纸，在中国古代民间形成了很多风俗。在立春时节，姑娘们将剪纸戴在头上作为装饰品，以此表达对于春天来临的快乐。而到了各类热闹节日，人们也爱将剪纸粘贴在走马灯或灯笼上，在灯光的衬托下，剪纸上的花纹更生动。民间剪纸题材大多来源于生活，剪纸创作者通过剪纸，表达的是对美好生活的向往。不论从造型特色还是艺术价值上看，剪纸都是具有魅力的中国民间手工艺品。

Paper-cutting is a craft that has been passed down in Chinese folklore for nearly a

thousand years. For skilled paper cutters, it is an improvised art. They have no paper to work with and can cut out countless designs with just a pair of scissors. And around paper-cutting, many customs were formed in ancient Chinese folklore. At the time of spring, girls wore paper cutouts on their heads as decorations to express their happiness at the arrival of spring. At festivals, paper-cutting were also used to decorate lanterns with rotating shadow figures or other lanterns, where the patterns on the paper-cutting were made more vivid by the light. Most of the folk paper-cutting themes come from life, and through paper-cutting, the creators express their aspirations for a better life. Whether in terms of stylistic features or artistic value, paper-cutting is an attractive Chinese folk craft.

3. 汉服　Hanfu

汉服是“汉民族传统服饰”的简称。汉服不仅仅指衣服，还包括头饰、足饰等多种装饰品在内。目前认为，汉服最早出现在殷商时期。大约在五千年前，中国出现了原始的农业和纺织业，开始用麻布做衣服，出现了汉服。

汉服在不同的朝代有着不同的样式和时尚。例如，汉代服饰主要特点为优雅；魏晋南北朝服饰的特点是自然；而到了唐代，襦裙（rúqún，这种服饰包括上身穿的短衣和下身束的裙子）深受女子喜爱，开始成为主流，服饰风格转向俏丽；宋代服饰在理学的影响下，回归简单、朴素。

在汉服的演变中，不变的是华夏民族对于礼仪的尊重。

Hanfu is the abbreviation for "traditional Han Chinese costume". Hanfu is not only clothing, but also includes a variety of decorative items such as headwear and footwear. It is now believed that Hanfu first appeared in the Yin and Shang dynasties. Around 5000 years ago, when primitive agriculture and weaving began in China, linen was used to make clothes and Hanfu emerged.

Hanfu had different styles and fashions in different dynasties. For example, the main characteristic of Han costume was elegance; in the Wei, Jin and Northern and Southern Dynasties the costume was characterized by its naturalness; while in the Tang Dynasty, Ruqun (rúqún, a costume consisting of a short garment worn on top and a skirt tied at the bottom) was popular with women and began to become mainstream, with the style of dress turning playful; and in the Song Dynasty the costume returned to simplicity and unadorned under the influence of the the Neo-Confucianism.

What has remained constant in the evolution of Chinese dress is the respect of the Chinese people for etiquette.

2 开始上课了 Class begins

热身 WARMING UP

生活中有很多“美”的事物，人很美、花很美、晚霞很美……在你眼里，什么是美的？

（王曼蓉 提供）

（华培烨 摄）

（高鑫 摄）

观看视频 WATCHING THE VIDEO

开始上课了，老师问同学们“美是什么”，同学们会怎么回答呢？

扫描视频二维码观看

内容提示 CONTENT TIPS

Part 1

课文 text

开始上课了

（上课前）

同学A：你们看见刘老师在群里发的阅读材料了吗？叫作《大希庇阿斯篇》。老师说，下节课要请几位同学讨论这篇文章，你们要报名吗？我觉得还挺有意思的。

（上课时）

刘老师：上了一天课，你又累又饿，急着去食堂吃饭。就在这个时候，一位老人在食堂的门口拦住了你，他说："同学，请问'美'是什么？"同学们，请问"美"是什么？

同学B：我认为美就是善良，善良就是好人。

同学C：我觉得美就是妈妈的脸。

同学D：我认为美就是好看。

同学A：同学们，我认为美就是我们自己，柏拉图说"美是难的"，因为认识你自己本身就是难的。

生词 new words

发 fā [v.] send, deliver

材料 cáiliào [n.] materials

大希庇阿斯篇 dàxībì'āsīpiān Great Hippias

讨论 tǎolùn [v.] discuss

篇 piān [mw.] a piece of writing

文章 wénzhāng [n.] article, essay

报名 bàomíng [v.] sign up

觉得 juéde [v.] feel, think

有意思 yǒuyìsi [adj.] interesting

拦住 lánzhù [n.] block

认为 rènwéi [v.] feel, think

善良 shànliáng [n.] kind-hearted, virtuous

认识 rènshi [v.] know, understand

本身 běnshēn [n.] itself, oneself

Part 2　注释 notes

1. 我觉得还挺有意思的。

副词“挺”，表示“很”的意思，常用结构“挺……的”。例如：

The adverb “挺” means “quite, rather” , similar to “很” . It is often used in the structure “挺……的” .For example:

① 这幅画挺好看的。

② 这家超市的东西挺便宜的，我经常来这儿买东西。

③ 这个房间又大又干净，我挺喜欢的。

2. 又累又饿

“又……又……”连接并列的形容词、动词或形容词短语、动词短语，表示两种动作、状态、情况同时存在。例如：

Structure “又……又……” is used to connect two adjectives, verbs or adjective phrases or verb phrases. It means the actions, states or situations exist at the same time. For example:

① 食堂的菜又便宜又好吃。

② 这个孩子又哭又叫，爸爸妈妈也没办法。

注意：我们不说“＊又很高又很大”或者“＊又高高的又大大的”。

Note：We can not say “＊又很高又很大” or “＊又高高的又大大的” .

3. 美是什么？

“是”字句一般表示判断，常见结构是“A ＋ 是 ＋ B”，否定形式是“A+ 不是 +B”。例如：

Usually, sentence with “是” (be) means a judgement. The usual structure is “A 是 B” . The negative one is “A+ 不是 +B” . For example:

① A：他是谁？

B：他是我爸爸。

② A：你是学生吗？

B：我不是学生。

4. 就在这个时候……

[副词]“就”常表示强调、肯定的语气，意思是“是这个，不是别的”。如：

[adv.] The word “就” implies the mood of emphasis and affirmative. It is this one, not others. For example:

① 他就是昨天来的。
② 我们就在这儿等你。

5. 时候

[名词] 表示某一段时间或某一时间点。可以用在疑问句询问时间。例如：

[n.] It indicates a certain period of time or a certain time point. It can be used to ask for time in an interrogative sentence. For example:

① 你什么时候起床？
② 我们什么时候上课？

也可以用在陈述句中表示某一段时间或某一时间点。例如：

It can also indicate time or a period of time in a declarative sentence. For example:

① 暑假的时候，我会去旅游。
② 没有课的时候，我会去图书馆。

"……的时候"也可以省略为"……时"。例如：

The expression "……的时候" can also be omitted as "……时". For example:

① 暑假时，我会去旅游。
② 没有课时，我会去图书馆。

6. 美是难的

"是……的"表示说话人对主语的看法、评价、说明或描述。例如：

"是……的" indicates the speaker's opinion, comment, explanation or description on the subject. For example:

① 他的话是对的。
② 这个答案是错的。
③ 明天是没有课的，我们可以去爬山。
④ 学习汉语，练习是非常重要的。

7. 美就是我们自己。

Beauty is within ourselves.

8. 认识你自己本身就是难的。

Knowing yourself in itself is hard.

综合练习　COMPREHENSIVE PRACTICE

Part 1　视频练习

看视频，判断对错　Watch the video and judge true or false

1. 视频的开头，同学 A 在用电脑写作业。 (　)
2. 美是指外表。 (　)
3. 同学 A 觉得刘老师发的阅读材料没意思。 (　)
4. 同学 B 认为美就是好看。 (　)
5. 同学们认为美是多种多样的。 (　)

看视频，选择填空　Watch the video and choose the best answer

1. 刘老师让同学们阅读了什么？ (　)

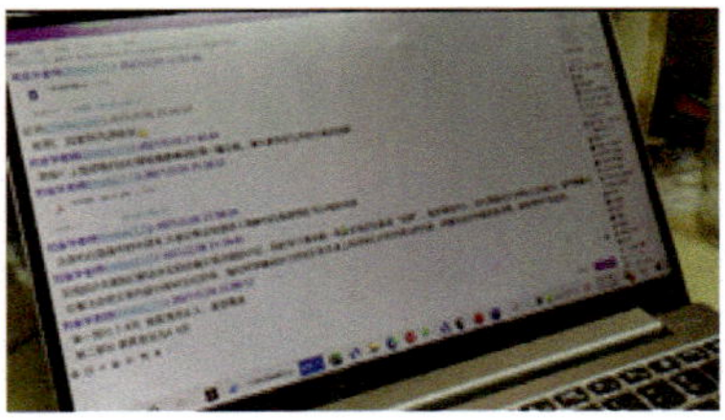

A. 小希庇阿斯篇　　B. 大希庇阿斯篇　　C. 查密迪斯篇

2. 同学们在讨论什么？ (　)

A. 丑是什么？　　B. 善是什么？　　C. 美是什么？

3. 同学 B 认为“美”是什么？ (　)

A．善良　　B. 温柔　　C. 勇敢

4. 同学 C 认为“美”是什么？ （　）

A．妈妈的笑　　B. 妈妈的手　　C. 妈妈的脸

5. 同学 D 认为“美”是什么？ （　）

A．好人　　B. 好看　　C. 好玩

看视频，回答问题 Watch the video and answer the questions

1. 同学 A 认为美是什么？为什么？
2. 大家认为同学 A 的观点是对的吗？为什么？

Part 2 书面练习

选词填空 Choose a word to fill in each blank

材料　　有意思　　讨论　　报名　　善良　　认为

1. 你会______今年的 HSK 三级的考试吗？
2. 我的奶奶很______，经常帮助有困难的人。
3. 杰克说那部电影很______，我们可以一起去看。
4. 请大家阅读老师发的______，下节课需要在课堂上______。
5. A：我觉得这本书很好看，你呢？
   B：我______一般。

完成句子 Complete the sentences

1. A：我每天都很忙。
   B：你每天都在做什么？
   A：______________。（又……又……）

2. A：这家饭店的菜怎么样？
　B：我觉得＿＿＿＿＿＿＿＿＿＿＿＿＿＿＿。（又……又……）
3. 夏天＿＿＿＿＿＿＿＿，不用穿很多衣服。（挺）
4. 这部电影我很喜欢，＿＿＿＿＿＿＿＿＿＿＿＿＿＿＿＿＿＿。（挺）
5. ＿＿＿＿＿＿＿＿＿，我去北京了。（……的时候）

从字到词　From Chinese characters to words

1. 阅读下面一段话，拿笔写一写“美”最开始的字形和现在的字形。

（甲骨文：美）

关于“美”字的来历，人们有两种解释：

① 看字形，人们认为由“羊”＋“大”组成。在古代，人们以羊肉为主要食物，羊大而肥美，就有了味道好、美味的意思。

② 看字形，人们认为是一个人，头上戴着羊角、牛角等装饰物，所以原来的意思就是漂亮、好看。

There are two explanations for the origin of the word “美”:

① Looking at the glyph, people think it is composed of “羊” + “大”. In ancient times, people used mutton as their main food. Sheep were big and fat, which meant delicious.

② Looking at the glyph, people think it is a person with horns of sheep and cattle on his head, so the original meaning is beautiful and good-looking.

（甲骨文）　　　　（现在的汉字）

2. 写出带“美”的词语，并用它来造句。

例如：（美好）生活是美好的。

（　　　）＿＿＿＿＿＿＿＿＿＿＿＿＿＿＿＿＿＿＿＿＿＿＿。

（　　　）＿＿＿＿＿＿＿＿＿＿＿＿＿＿＿＿＿＿＿＿＿＿＿。

（　　　）＿＿＿＿＿＿＿＿＿＿＿＿＿＿＿＿＿＿＿＿＿＿＿。

Part 3 拓展练习

口语表达 Oral expression

同学们，你们注意到视频里的老师和同学们课下沟通的时候用的是什么 APP 吗？在你的国家，你们用什么 APP 进行沟通呢？和大家说一说。

复述课文 Repeat the text

上课前，刘老师在班级群里……，叫作……，还说下节课……。同学 A 觉得……，问大家……。

上课的时候，刘老师问同学们……，同学们开始了讨论。

同学 B 说……，……就是……。同学 C 觉得美是……，同学 D 认为美是……。

最后，同学 A 认为美就是……，柏拉图说……，因为……。大家认为她说的是……的。

小组活动 Group work

3~4 人一组，首先提出和“美”有关的任意观点，组内同学都谈谈自己的看法，在下面表格中记录下来，然后每组请一位同学报告本小组的讨论结果。

记录表：

观点：________认为 / 觉得________。		
小组成员	看法	原因（举例）
杰克	男性和女性现在都可以用“美”来形容。	

文化链接 CULTURAL LINK

1. 腾讯 QQ Tencent QQ

QQ 是基于互联网的即时通讯软件，1999 年腾讯推出，标志是一只戴着红色围巾的小企鹅。QQ 支持在线聊天、视频聊天及语音聊天、共享文件、远程控制、QQ 邮箱、传送离线文件、存储文件等多种功能，使用便捷，在人们的工作和学

习中十分受欢迎。

同时，QQ 空间还具有博客（blog）的功能，QQ 用户可以在上面发表动态，展示自己的生活点滴等，非常受人们欢迎。调查显示，自微信普及后，QQ 的常用用户主要是青少年。QQ 也是中国学校最常用的沟通软件。

QQ is an internet-based instant messaging APP launched by Tencent in 1999, with the logo of a little penguin wearing a red scarf. QQ supports online chat, video chat, voice chat, file sharing, remote control, QQ mailbox, offline file transfer, file storage and other functions. QQ is easy to use. It is very popular among people while working and studying.

At the same time, Qzone has also a function of the blog. QQ users can post things in the Qzone, displaying every bit of their lives and so on. Qzone is very popular among people. According to the survey, since WeChat has gained its popularity, teenagers become QQ' s regular users. QQ is also the most commonly used communication software in Chinese schools.

2. 微信 WeChat

微信是当下中国最受欢迎的一款通讯 APP，普及度很高。对于很多中国人来说，它不仅仅是一款简单的聊天工具，它更是一个多功能平台。

作为社交工具，微信可以发语音、文字消息、文件、表情包等，也支持语音、视频通话，还可以让人们在朋友圈分享生活点滴。作为娱乐工具，通过订阅公众号，人们可以关注自己感兴趣的博主，看新闻等；通过视频号，人们可以浏览有趣的短视频；游戏中心还支持和微信好友进行游戏互动。最重要的是作为支付工具，微信支付和支付宝作为中国两大支付方式，改变了人们的生活。微信好友之间可以发微信红包、微信转账；乘坐交通工具、医院缴费、出门逛街等可以使用微信支付。

微信方便了人们的生活，生活缴费、看病挂号、景点预约、点菜买单等都可以在手机上用微信完成。可以说，微信已经成为中国人生活方式的重要组成部分。

WeChat is the most popular instant message APP in China, which enjoys a high popularity. For most

Chinese, WeChat is more than a simple tool for chatting. It is also a multi-functional platform.

As a tool for socialization, WeChat can be used to send voice messages, text messages, files, emojis, etc. It also supports voice calls and video calls. People can share their lives with friends in WeChat moments. As an entertainment tool, WeChat allows you to follow the bloggers you are interested in and get some news, if you have subscribed to related public accounts. Through the video ID, you can browse interesting short videos; You can also play games together with your friends at the game center. Most importantly, as payment tools, WeChat Pay and Alipay, the two major payment methods in China, have changed people's lives. WeChat friends can send WeChat red envelopes, do WeChat transfer; WeChat payment can be used for paying for transportation, hospital and shopping.

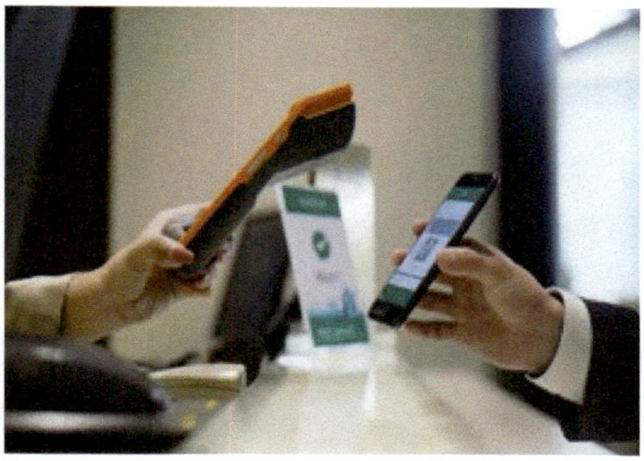

Life is easier with WeChat. Utilities, fees for making medical registrations or scenic spot appointments, and bills in restaurants, along with other things can be paid via WeChat on your mobile phone. It can be said that WeChat has become an important part of Chinese people's way of life.

3 今天吃什么？
What to eat today？

热身　WARMING UP

中国的美食多种多样，有热辣的重庆火锅、香喷喷的北京烤鸭、酸酸甜甜的糖醋排骨……你喜欢吃什么中国菜呢？

重庆火锅

北京烤鸭

糖醋里脊

观看视频　WATCHING THE VIDEO

俗话说“民以食为天”，人们每天都在思考“今天吃什么”……让我们一起来看看同学A和同学B的一天都吃了什么吧！

扫描视频二维码观看

内容提示 CONTENT TIPS

Part 1

课文 text

今天吃什么

（早上）

同学A：早餐你想吃什么？

同学B：我想要一个肉包和一个茶叶蛋，你呢？

同学A：我想要一杯豆浆和一根油条。

（中午）

同学B：我昨天中午吃了西餐，今天想吃中国菜，你有什么推荐的吗？

同学A：我觉得川菜很好吃，你可以去试试。

同学B：川菜是不是很辣？我不能吃辣，还有别的吗？

同学A：是的，川菜比较辣。你还可以去快餐窗口看看，那里的菜不但种类多，而且价格便宜。

同学B：好的，我去看看。

同学A：明天我想尝尝西餐，你有什么建议吗？

同学B：我喜欢吃黑椒口味的意面，还有牛排。你可以试试。

生词 new words

早餐 zǎocān [n.] breakfast

肉包 ròubāo [n.] pork bun, meat bun

茶叶蛋 cháyèdàn [n.] eggs stewed in tea

豆浆 dòujiāng [n.] soya–bean milk

油条 yóutiáo [n.] deep–fried dough sticks

西餐 xīcān [n.] Western–style food

推荐 tuījiàn [v.] recommend

川菜 chuāncài [n.] Sichuan dishes

辣 là [adj.] peppery, pungent, hot

快餐 kuàicān [n.] fast food

窗口 chuāngkǒu [n.] window, wicket

种类 zhǒnglèi [n.] kind, sort, type

价格 jiàgé [n.] price

便宜 pián・yi [adj.] cheap, inexpensive

建议 jiànyì [n.] proposal, suggestion

黑椒口味 hēijiāo kǒuwèi [n.] black pepper flavor

意面 yìmiàn [n.] pasta

牛排 niúpái [n.] beefsteak

（晚上）

同学B：你晚上怎么吃得这么少？最近在减肥吗？

减肥 jiǎnféi [v.] reduce weight

同学A：不是的，我晚上习惯少吃点。因为中国人常说“早上吃得好，中午吃得饱，晚上吃得少”。

习惯 xíguàn [n.] habit, custom

同学B：原来是这样啊。以后我晚上也要少吃点，还能顺便减肥呢！

顺便 shùnbiàn [adv.] conveniently, in passing

Part 2　注释　notes

1. 你有什么推荐的吗？/你有什么建议吗？

What do you recommend? / Do you have any suggestions?

这些都是用来询问建议的句子，可以用“我觉得……不错，你可以试试”来回答。例如：

These are sentences for asking for advice. You can answer with “我觉得……不错，你可以试试”. For example:

① A：周末我想出去玩，你有什么推荐的地方吗？
B：我觉得去博物馆不错，你可以去试试。

② A：我想买个礼物送给妈妈，你有什么建议吗？
B：我觉得送花很不错，你可以试试。

2. 试试

汉语里有些动词可以重叠，表示动作经历的时间短或轻松、随便；有时也表示尝试或有礼貌。单音节动词重叠的形式是“AA”或“A一A”，如“看一看”“听一听”“说一说”。例如：

In Chinese, some verbs can be reduplicated to indicate an action is short, easy or casual; sometimes it also indicates a try or shows courtesy. The reduplicative form of a monosyllabic verb is “AA” or “A一A”, for example, “看一看”, “听一听”, “说一说”. For example:

① 我能看看你的书吗？

② 我想试试新手机。

③ 我们来听一听这句话。

④ 大家一起来说一说。

动词重叠后不能再带补语。我们不说“我看看一下”。

If a verb is reduplicated, it is not followed by a complement. “我看看一下” is wrong.

3. 川菜是不是很辣？

用“是不是”提问的句子表示问话人对某事已经有了比较肯定的估计，但是需要得到进一步证实。“是不是”可以在谓语前，也可以在句首或句尾。例如：

A question with “是不是” implies that the questioner has formed a relatively affirmative answer that needs a further confirmation. “是不是” may come before the predicate, at the beginning or the end of the sentence. For example:

① A：山姆是不是搬家了？
B：是的。

② A：是不是老师让你写作业？
B：是的。

③ A：你不喜欢喝咖啡，是不是？
B：是的，我不喜欢喝咖啡。

4. 那里的菜不但种类多，而且价格便宜。

“不但……而且……”，连接两个分句，表示递进关系。“不但”用在第一个分句，常和“而且 / 还 / 也”等配合使用。例如：

“不但……而且……” meaning “not only… but also ...”, joins two clauses to show a progressive relationship. “不但” is used in the first clause, and is usually used together with “而且 / 还 / 也”. For example:

① 这家超市的水果不但新鲜，而且便宜。

② 他不但会说英语，还会说日语。

③ 她不但是我们的老师，还是我们的朋友。

注意：两个分句主语相同，“不但”用在主语后；两个分句主语不同，“不但”用在主语前。“不但”位置不同，句子意思也不同。例如：

Note: If the two clauses share one subject, “不但” is placed after the subject; if the two clauses have different subjects, “不但” is placed before the first subject. When it is placed in different positions, sentence indicate different meanings. For example:

① 艾玛不但会唱歌，也会跳舞。

② 不但艾玛会唱歌，安娜也会唱歌。

5. 早上吃得好，中午吃得饱，晚上吃得少。

这句话是中国的俗语。意思是：早上吃的早餐要有营养，中午的午餐要多吃一些，晚上的晚餐要少吃一些。

This sentence is a Chinese proverb. It means: breakfast in the morning should be nutritious, lunch at noon should be more, and dinner at night should be less.

"吃得好、吃得饱、吃得少"中的"好、饱、少"是情态补语。情态补语表示对动作、状态的描写或评价。汉语中，可以用"得"构成状态补语，描写某种状态。"得"前一般是动词，"得"后一般是形容词。例如：

A complement of state describes or evaluates an action or the state of an affair. In Chinese, "得" can be used to form a complement to describe a certain state. Usually "得" is preceded by a verb and followed by an adjective. For example:

S	V	得	Adj.①
小明	跑	得	快
丽丽	唱	得	很好
大家	玩儿	得	很高兴

6. 原来是这样啊。

[副词]表示"发现了以前不知道的情况"，用在主语前面或后面都可以。例如：

[adv.] It can indicate the discovery of a formerly unknown situation. It can be used either before or after the subject. For example:

① 我之前以为她是韩国人，今天才发现原来她是日本人。
② 这本书我找了很久都没找到，原来是你拿走了。
③ 我以为今天是星期四，原来是我记错了。

综合练习　COMPREHENSIVE PRACTICE

Part 1　视频练习

看视频，判断对错　Watch the video and judge true or false

1. 同学A很喜欢吃肉包和茶叶蛋。　　(　　)

---

① Adj. 代表形容词，下同。

2. 同学 B 昨天晚上吃了西餐。 （ ）
3. 川菜比较辣。 （ ）
4. 同学 A 不能吃辣。 （ ）
5. 同学 B 晚上吃得很少。 （ ）

看视频，选择填空 Watch the video and choose the best answer

1. 同学 A 早餐吃了什么？ （ ）
   A. 肉包和茶叶蛋　　B. 豆浆和油条　　C. 豆浆和肉包
2. 同学 A 最后推荐同学 B 去______吃午餐，因为________。 （ ）
   A. 川菜馆；那里的菜不但价格便宜，而且好吃。
   B. 快餐窗口；那里的菜不但种类多，而且价格便宜。
   C. 快餐窗口；那里的菜不但好吃，而且价格便宜。
3. 同学 B 喜欢吃什么西餐？ （ ）
   A. 汉堡和薯条　　B. 牛排和三明治　　C. 牛排和意面
4. 同学 B 下次会怎么吃晚餐？ （ ）
   A. 少吃一点　　B. 不吃晚餐　　C. 多吃一点

看视频，回答问题 Watch the video and answer the questions

1. 同学 A 推荐了哪些中国菜？
2. 同学 B 去吃川菜了吗？为什么？
3. 为什么同学 A 晚上吃得很少？

Part 2 书面练习

选词填空 Choose a word to fill in each blank

价格　便宜　种类　顺便　习惯　推荐　口味

1. A：我最近想买衣服，你有什么________的吗？
   B：我上次逛的那家店很不错，________也不贵，你可以去看看。
2. 我们去吃饭吧，回来的路上________去图书馆借书。
3. A：今天周六，你怎么这么早就起床了？
   B：我________早起去跑步。
4. A：哇！这家店的蛋糕________很多，你想要哪种？
   B：我要巧克力________的。
5. 这里的水果很________。

完成句子 Complete the sentences

1. A：你的舍友会说汉语吗？
   B：他不仅会说，而且________________。（得）
2. A：今天教室怎么没人啊？
   B：今天是周末，不上课。
   A：____________。（原来）
3. A：我不知道怎么去图书馆。
   B：你可以____________。（VV / V 一 V）
4. A：今天天气____________？（是不是）
   B：是的，我们不能出门了。
5. A：假期快到了，你____________？（是不是）
   B：是的，我已经买好票了。

连词成句 Match the words into a sentence

1. 不但 唱歌 喜欢 玛丽 跳舞 而且 喜欢

____

2. 运动员 还是 杰克 不但 作家 是

____

3. 云南 好吃 不但 很 风景 食物 也 美 很

____

4. 安娜 不但 唱歌 会 玛丽 唱歌 也 而且 会

____

5. 不但 中国菜 会做 我 也 我的朋友 会做

____

Part 3 拓展练习

双人活动 Pair work

两人一组，根据情景要求进行对话，A 询求建议，B 给出建议。

情景：

① 卡特过生日要送什么礼物？

② 可以去哪里旅游？

③ 大学毕业后是工作还是读研究生？

提示：

询求建议的句子：	提出建议的句子：
你有什么要推荐的吗？	我觉得……不错，你可以试试。
你有什么建议吗？	我建议你……。
你有什么好建议？	你为什么不试试……呢？
你说，我应该怎么做呢？	我觉得你最好不要……。
你觉得我应该怎么做？	我认为你不应该……。

复述课文 Repeat the text

（早上）

同学A：早餐你……？

同学B：我想要……和……，你呢？

同学A：我想要……和……。

（中午）

同学B：我昨天中午吃了……，今天想吃……，你……？

同学A：我觉得……，你可以……。

同学B：川菜……？我不能……，还有别的吗？

同学A：是的，川菜……。你还可以去……看看，那里的菜不但……，而且……。

同学B：好的，我……。

同学A：明天我想……，你……？

同学B：我喜欢吃……的……，还有……。你可以……。

（晚上）

同学B：你晚上怎么……？最近在……吗？

同学A：不是的，我晚上……。因为中国人常说“早上……，中午……，晚上……”。

同学B：原来……啊。以后我晚上……，还能……呢！

口语表达 Oral expression

1. 你的家乡有哪些美食？它们的味道怎么样？
2. 你觉得中餐和西餐有什么区别？

文化链接　CULTURAL LINK

1.“民以食为天”成语故事

The Chinese idiom story: “Food is the order of the day for the people”

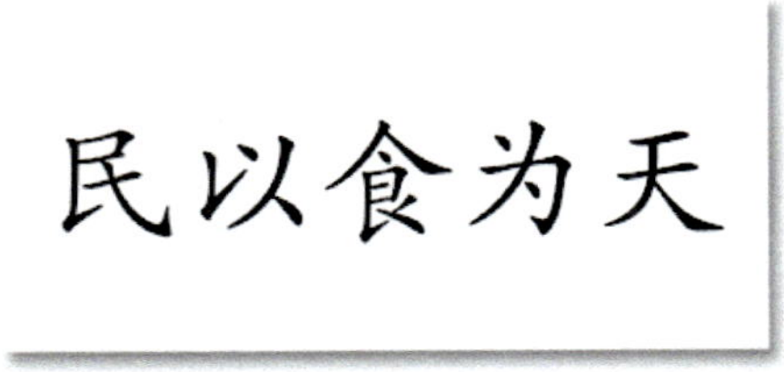

传说在秦朝末年，刘邦和项羽两大集团争夺政权。刘邦正守在荥阳（xíngyáng，地名，今位于河南省），荥阳地区山上有一座小城，城内有储藏食物的仓库。由于刘邦在和项羽的几次战斗中没有取得胜利，他决定放弃这个地区。他的谋士（móushì，拥有智慧的人才）劝说他：“作为能够做大事的王者，您应该把老百姓看作是自己的天，而百姓又把食物当作自己的天。现在，山上的小城中有储藏粮食的仓库，得到这块地的人是能得到百姓忠心的人啊！”刘邦听了他的话，继续坚守这块土地，并最终取得了战争的胜利。“民以食为天”的意思是食物对于百姓来说是非常重要的。

Legend has it that at the end of the Qin Dynasty, two groups, Liu Bang and Xiang Yu, were fighting for power. Liu Bang was defending Xingyang (xíngyáng, the name of the place, now in Henan Province), a small city on a hill in the area of Xingyang with warehouses for storing food. As Liu Bang had failed to win several battles against Xiang Yu, he decided to abandon the area. His strategists (móushì, talents with wisdom) advised him: "As a king capable of doing great things, you should regard the people as your own heaven, and the people in turn regard food as their own heaven. Now, there are storehouses for storing grain in the little city on the hill, and the man who gets this land is the one who can gain the loyalty of the people!" Liu Bang listened to him, continued to hold on to the land, and eventually won the war. " This means that food is very important to the people.

2. 中国八大菜系

The eight major Chinese cuisines

中国各个地区的气候、地形、历史、饮食习惯不同，这导致地方菜品有各自的特色和风味。一般来说，中国八大菜系指的是鲁菜、川菜、粤菜、苏菜、闽菜、浙菜、徽菜和湘菜，这是根据地区划分的，并用代表省的简称来命名。八大菜系之间有不同，也有相似之处。比如，湘菜口味偏辣，而苏菜则口味清淡。但在做菜的方式上，湘菜和苏菜又采用了一些相同的手艺，比如煨（wēi，用火加热烘干、烤熟），像煨鸡是江苏常熟地区的传统名菜，而经典的煨牛肉则出自湖南地区，它们的工艺是一样的，但所属菜系不同，在食材呈现上就是完全不同的了。

（张峰 摄）

（张峰 摄）

Different regions of China have different climates, topography, histories and eating habits, which have led to regional cuisines with their own characteristics and flavours. Generally speaking, the eight major Chinese cuisines refer to Lu, Sichuan, Guangdong, Jiangsu, Fujian, Zhejiang, Huizhou and Hunan, which are divided according to region and named with the abbreviation of the representative province. There are differences as well as similarities between the eight major cuisines. For example, Hunan cuisine has a spicy flavour, while Suzhou cuisine is light. However, in the way they are prepared, Hunan and Suzhou cuisines use some of the same techniques, such as simmering (wēi), which is a traditional dish from the Changshu region of Jiangsu, and the classic simmered beef, which comes from the Hunan region, but with different cuisine families, the presentation of the ingredients is completely different.

4 你在哪儿？
Where are you ?

热身　WARMING UP

同学们，来到校园这么久，你们都熟悉校园了吗？介绍一下你熟悉的“校园一角”吧！

观看视频　WATCHING THE VIDEO

同学 A 和同学 B 约好一起去上课，他们能顺利汇合吗？让我们一起来看看吧！

扫描视频二维码观看

内容提示 CONTENT TIPS

Part 1

课文 text	生词 new words
你在哪儿？	
（同学 A 和同学 B 在打电话）	
同学A：喂，我们一起去教室上课吧？	
同学B：好呀。	
同学A：你现在在哪儿？我去找你吧。	
同学B：我在宿舍。	宿舍 sùshè [n.] dormitory
同学A：你的宿舍在哪儿？	
同学B：在晖园12栋。	晖园 huīyuán [n.] name of a dormitory area
同学A：知道了，你在宿舍等一下。	栋 dòng [m.n.] a building
（同学 A 和同学 B 见面了）	
同学B：我们今天在哪儿上课？	
同学A：在文德楼301，今天上的是文化课"中国民居"。	文德楼 wéndélóu [n.] Wende building 民居 mínjū [n.] residential houses
同学B：中国民居？那你的家乡在哪儿？	家乡 jiāxiāng [n.] hometown, homeplace
同学A：我家在北京。	
同学B：哦~我知道北京有四合院。	四合院 sìhéyuàn [n.] Quadrangle Dwellings in Beijing
同学A：那你家呢？	建筑 jiànzhù [n.] building, structure
同学B：我家在苏州，你了解苏州的建筑吗？	苏州园林 sūzhōu yuánlín [n.] Classical Gardens of Suzhou
同学A：听说苏州园林很有名，真想去见识见识。	有名 yǒumíng [adj.] well-known, famous 见识 jiàn · shi [v.] enrich one's experience

同学B：有机会的话，我们一起去苏州玩儿！

同学A：好呀，一言为定！

机会 jīhuì [n.] chance, opportunity

一言为定 yìyán-wéidìng A promise is a promise

Part 2 注释 notes

1. 你现在在哪儿？

“现在”是时间词。时间词在句子中做状语，经常出现在主语后边。例如：

“现在” is a time word. When a time word serves as an adverbial modifier in a sentence, it often follows the subject. For example:

S	时间词	V
我们	八点	上课
杰夫	晚上十一点	睡觉
他	明天	去上海

“在”是动词，后边加上表示位置的词语做句子的谓语，用于指示人或者事物的位置。例如：

“在” is a verb. When it is followed by a word of locality and acts as the predicate of a sentence, it indicates the location of somebody or something. For example:

S	在	地点
我	在	家
我家	在	南京
我的书	在	教室

“哪儿”是疑问代词，用在疑问句中，询问人或事物的位置。例如：

The interrogative pronoun “哪儿” is used to ask about the location of somebody or something. For example:

① 老师在哪儿？

② 你的宿舍在哪儿？

③ 你的杯子在哪儿？

2. 我们今天在哪儿上课？

“在”也是介词，后边加上表示位置的词语，用于介绍动作行为发生的位置。

例如：

“在” can also act as a preposition, used before a word of locality to introduce the place where an action or behavior takes place. For example:

S	在	地点	V
我	在	家	看书
他们	在	超市	买东西
我朋友	在	医院	工作

3. 你在宿舍**等一下**。

“V＋一下”表示时间短暂，也表示做一次或者试着做的意思。例如：

“一下” is used after a verb, indicating a short moment. Sometimes it also means "for once" or "have a try". For example:

S	V	一下	O
我	休息	一下	
我	看	一下	
我	问	一下	老师
你	读	一下	课文

4. **那你**家**呢**？

“那你……呢”句式可以用在省略疑问句中，疑问的内容可以根据上下文来判断。例如：

“那你……呢” is here used in an abbreviated interrogative sentence where the question can be deduced from the context. For example:

① 我的家乡在北京，那你家呢？ ＝我的家乡在北京，那你家在哪儿？

② A：我今年二十岁了，那你呢？
B：我二十一岁了。

③ A：这次考试我的成绩是 88 分，那你的成绩呢？
B：我的是 89 分。

5. **听说**苏州园林很有名……

“听说……”表示“听别人说……”，强调听到了一些事情。例如：

“听说……” means "I heard that…" or "It is said that…". It emphasizes that one has heard some news or information. For example:

① A：李娜今天怎么没来上课？
　B：听说她生病了。

② 听说明天放假，同学们都很高兴。

③ 我听说他已经回家了。

6. 有机会的话，我们一起去苏州玩儿。

“有机会的话……”表示在未来自己有时间就会去做这件事。例如：

“有机会的话” means that in the future, if one has the time, they will do the thing mentioned in context. For example:

① A：我好想去游泳啊。
　B：这周末有机会的话，我们可以一起去。

② 艾伦很喜欢中国，有机会的话他一定会来中国旅游。

③ 有机会的话，我们会再见面的。

“我们一起去苏州玩儿”是连动句，有两个谓语动词“去”和“玩儿”。连动句的谓语由两个或两个以上的动词短语构成，它们之间没有停顿，也不使用关联词语。例如：

“我们一起去苏州玩儿” is a multi-verb sentence, which contains two predicate verbs “去” and “玩儿”。The predicate of a multi-verb sentence consists of two or more verb phrases. Those verb phrases are contiguous parts with no pause or conjunction in between. For example:

① 他来中国学习汉语。

② 我们去电影院看电影。

③ 我走路去上课。

7. 一言为定

成语。意思是“一句话说定了，不再更改”。比喻说话算数，决不反悔。例如：

Idiom. It means "one sentence is settled, no change". Metaphor: keep your word and never repent. For example:

① A：我们明年一起出国留学吧。
　B：好呀，一言为定。

② A：我们明天晚上八点在校门口见面。
　B：一言为定，你可不要迟到哦。

综合练习 COMPREHENSIVE PRACTICE

Part 1 视频练习

看视频，判断对错 Watch the video and judge true or false

1. 同学 A 和同学 B 要一起去图书馆。 (   )
2. 同学 B 在宿舍楼下等同学 A。 (   )
3. 同学 A 和同学 B 今天上的是文化课。 (   )
4. 同学 B 一点儿也不了解北京。 (   )
5. 同学 A 已经去过苏州了。 (   )

看视频，选择填空 Watch the video and choose the best answer

1. 同学 A 打电话的时候，同学 B 在______，位置是______。 (   )
   A. 宿舍楼里；晖园 13 栋
   B. 宿舍楼下；军园 12 栋
   C. 宿舍楼里；晖园 12 栋
2. 同学 A 和同学 B 今天在______上课，上课内容是______。 (   )
   A. 文德楼；中国建筑
   B. 文德楼；中国民居
   C. 明德楼；中国民居
3. 同学 A 的家乡是______，著名的建筑有______。 (   )
   A. 北京；四合院
   B. 南京；四合院
   C. 北京；乔家大院
4. 根据视频，苏州的______很有名。 (   )
   A. 楼阁　　B. 院落　　C. 园林

看视频，回答问题 Watch the video and answer the questions

1. 同学 B 的家乡在哪儿？同学 A 知道了后，有什么反应？
2. 视频的最后，同学 A 和同学 B 约定了什么？

Part 2 书面练习

选词填空 Choose a word to fill in each blank

宿舍　家乡　建筑　见识　机会　一言为定　有名

1. A：暑假有________的话，我们一起去旅游吧！
   B：好啊，________。
2. 已经十一点半了，________要关门了，安娜还没回来。
3. 我的________是云南，那里山美，水美，人更美。
4. A：我上周去了北京，还拍了很多照片。
   B：听说北京故宫很________，我想去________一下。
5. 哈法利塔是世界上最高的________，有 828 米。

完成句子 Complete the sentences

1. A：我看见你发在朋友圈的照片了，大海真美呀！
   B：______________________________。（有机会的话……）
2. A：______________________________。（那你……呢？）
   B：我的学校也会提供宿舍。
3. A：下课了，我们一起去商场逛街吧！
   B：我很累，____________。（V +一下）
4. A：__________________，你想去看看吗？（听说）
   B：好呀，我们可以周六一起去。
5. A：__________________？（哪儿）
   B：我现在在家。
   A：大家在操场做什么呀？
   B：明天就要体育考试了，____________________。（在）

连词成句 Match the words into a sentence

1. 去 下周 一起 我们 野餐 公园 吧

____

2. 明天 要 图书馆 学习 我 去

____

3. 安娜 上学 自行车 骑

____

4. 杰克 电脑 作业 用 写

____

5. 后 放学 要 休息 我 回家

____

Part 3　拓展练习

口语表达　Oral expression

用本课所学语言点，向同学们简要介绍一下你的一天。

提示：时间状语、连动句、听说、V+ 一下……

例如：

周六，我早上八点起床，然后去食堂吃早餐。吃完早餐，我就和朋友去图书馆学习。中午的时候，朋友说："听说最近新上映了一部好看的电影，我们一起去看看吧。"我也想休息一下，所以我们就一起去商场看电影了……

复述课文　Repeat the text

（同学 A 和同学 B 在打电话）

同学A：喂，XXX，我们一起……吧？

同学B：好呀。

同学A：你现在……？ 我去……吧。

同学B：我在……。

同学A：……在……？

同学B：在……12栋。

同学A：知道了，你在宿舍……。

（同学 A 和同学 B 见面了）

同学B：我们……在哪儿……？

同学A：在……301，今天上的是……"中国……"。

同学B：……？ 那你的……在哪儿？

同学A：我家……。

同学B：哦~我知道……有……。

同学A：那……呢？

同学B：我家……，你了解……的……吗？

同学A：听说……很有名，真想去……。

同学B：……，我们一起……！

同学A：好呀，……！

小组活动 Group work

3~4人一组，互相介绍自己的家乡及家乡的特色建筑，每组请一位同学报告情况。

例如：

A：我的家乡在福建，你家呢？

B：我家在……。福建特色建筑是什么？

A：福建土楼很有名，你们家乡的建筑呢？

B：……。

记录表：

	名字	家乡	建筑
1	李丽	中国福建	土楼

文化链接 CULTURAL LINK

1. 中国民居 Chinese residence

民居是建筑中最早出现的类型，是中国建筑史上对“民间居住建筑物”的习惯称呼，作为住房的民居在人们的日常生活中占有非常重要的位置。

中国的民居建筑是千百年来劳动人民用自己勤劳智慧的双手，在适应与改造大自然的漫长岁月中创造出来的。由于中国幅员广阔，各地区的自然地理条件不同，56个民族风格与传统各异，生产和生活建筑多姿多彩，富有创造性。

Residential house is the earliest type of architecture, and it is the customary name for "civil residential buildings" in the history of Chinese architecture. Residential houses as housing occupy a very important position in Chinese daily life.

The residential buildings in China are created by the working people for thousands of years with their industrious and intelligent hands, in the long years of adapting and transforming nature. Due to the vast territory of China and the different natural and geographical conditions in different regions, the 56 ethnic groups have different styles and traditions, and their production and living buildings are colorful and creative.

2. 北方民居 Northern residence

北方地区冬季漫长，气候相对寒冷；平原众多，用地相对宽松，地形平整、单一；民风也比南方淳朴、粗犷。

The northern region of winter is long, the climate is relatively cold, the plains are numerous, the land is relatively loose, the terrain is flat, single, and the folk custom is also more simple and rough than the south.

东北民居：

（东北三省：吉林、辽宁、黑龙江）以吉林的蒙古族马架房为代表。在山墙开山，形如吉林东部山区汉族农民使用的马架，故称马架房。其房平面近方形，上部可用椭圆顶，极似蒙古包，保持了蒙古族的民族习惯。

Northeast China residence: (three provinces in northeast China: Jilin, Liaoning and Heilongjiang) They are represented by the Mongolian horse-frame residences in Jilin. In the gable mountain, such as the shape of the han Chinese farmers in the mountains of eastern Jilin, so called the horse frame residence. The upper part of the room plane can be used nearly square ellipse top, very similar to yurts, to maintain the Mongolian national habits.

北京民居：

以四合院为代表，四合院式的住房是中国最为普遍、历史最为久远的住宅形式。四合院是由四面房屋围合起来，大门是等级和地位的象征，往往有着华丽的装饰，以表达四合院主人对生活的美好愿望。

Beijing residence: represented by the quadrangle courtyard, the quadrangle courtyard housing is the most common and the oldest residential form in China. Siheyuan is surrounded by four sides of the residence, the gate is a symbol of rank and status, often with ornate decoration, to express the Siheyuan owner's good wishes for life.

陕北民居：

以窑洞为代表。黄土高原气候干旱，土地以黄土质地为主，土质疏松易于挖掘，故当地人民因地制宜创造性地挖洞而居，不仅节省建筑材料，而且具有冬暖夏凉的优越性。

Northern Shaanxi residence: cave dwellings are representative. The loess Plateau has a dry climate and is dominated by loess. The loose soil is easy to dig, so the local people adopt creative measures to dig holes and live in the loess Plateau, which not only saves building materials, but also has the advantage of being warm in winter and cool in summer.

山西民居：

以土坯大砖为建筑材料，常为瓦房。瓦房的布局、结构一般以三间为主，院墙和房屋形成四合院。最出名的是乔家大院，是山西省集中反映晋中地区民俗的博物馆。

Shanxi residence: adobe bricks as building materials, often tile-roofed residences. Tile-roofed residence layout, structure is generally three-based, courtyard walls and residences form a Siheyuan. The most famous is the Qiao family courtyard, which is a museum that reflects the folk customs of JinZhong area in Shanxi Province.

3. 南方民居 Southern residence

南方地区气候炎热，用地狭窄，丘陵、平原相间，建筑材料丰富多样，民居建筑的总体风格是清新、通透。民居建筑平面比较规整，庭院很小，房屋高大。因为多雨天，屋顶坡度陡峻。

The southern region has a hot climate, narrow land, alternating hills and plains, rich and diverse building materials, and the overall style of residential buildings is fresh and transparent. The residential building plane is orderly, the courtyard is small, the residence is tall. Because it is rainy, the roof slope is steep.

江苏民居：

气候温和、河流众多，城镇及乡村民居大都利用地形邻河依水而建。住房布局紧凑，一般为两层楼房并建有楼阁。房层高、门窗高大，利于通风，外观朴素、粉墙灰瓦形成独特的水乡人家。

Jiangsu residence: the climate is mild and there are many rivers. Most of the town and country folk residences are built along the river by the topography. The housing layout is compact, usually two-storey buildings with pavilions. Room height, doors and windows tall, conducive to ventilation, simple appearance, white wall gray tiles form a unique family.

上海民居：

上海旧的住宅除一部分花园楼外，以里弄“石库门”房子最具代表性。大片住宅成排布置，建筑布局紧凑，高2～3层，青瓦坡屋顶，并有小型晒台。

Shanghai residence: in addition to some garden buildings, Shikumen residences in the inner lane are the most representative. Large residences are arranged in rows, with a compact architectural layout, two or three stories high, green tile slope roof, and small terrace.

安徽民居：

以“天井”为代表，其实就是较小的院落。中国南方炎热多雨而潮湿，人稠山多地窄，所以布局密集而多楼房。天井民居以长方形天井为中心，周高墙围护，外面几乎看不到瓦，只有狭长的天井采光、通风与外界沟通。雨天落下的雨水从四面屋顶流入天井，俗称“四水归堂”，也反映了徽商“肥水不流外田”的心态。

（刘丰果　摄）

（刘丰果　摄）

Anhui residence: represented by "courtyard", they are actually smaller courtyards. South China is hot, rainy and humid, densely populated, hilly and narrow, so the layout is dense and has many buildings. Courtyard Dwellings are centered on horizontal and rectangular courtyards, surrounded by high walls. Tile can hardly be seen outside, and only long narrow courtyards are used for lighting, ventilation and communication with the outside world. In rainy days, the rain water flows into the patio from the four roofs, commonly known as "four waters return to the hall", which also reflects the mentality of Huizhou merchants that "fertile water does not flow to the fields outside".

福建民居：

以客家人土楼为代表，是一种特殊农村住宅。土楼外形有方、圆之分，酷似庞大碉堡，外墙厚 1 米，可达 5 层高；房间总数可达 300 余间，同族数百人筑土楼而居。福建处于沿海地带，坚固的土楼既能防御海上盗贼，又能防震、防潮、保暖隔热。

Fujian residence: hakka tulou is a kind of special rural residence. The tulou are square or round in shape, resembling a huge bunker. The outer walls are one meter thick and up to five stories high. The total number of rooms was more than 300, and hundreds of people of the same clan lived in earthen buildings. Fujian is located in the coastal area, and the strong tulou can not only protect against thieves at sea, but also protect against shock, moisture and heat.

云南民居：

云南特色建筑为傣族竹楼，全部用竹子和茅草筑成，分上下两层。下层四周无遮拦，用来饲养牲畜家禽，堆放杂物。上层铺设竹板，四周围有竹篱，房顶用草排覆盖，带有栏杆、走廊。

Yunnan residence: The traditional bamboo house is a characteristic building of the Dai nationality. It is made of bamboo and thatch, and has two floors. The lower layer around the enclosure, used to feed livestock and poultry, stacked sundries. The upper layer is lined with bamboo, surrounded by bamboo hedges, and the roof is covered with grass rows, with railings and corridors.

第二单元　校园活动篇
Unit 2　Campus Activities

5 有意思的体育课
Interesting PE classes

热身 WARMING UP

同学们，你们喜欢运动吗？你们的体育课都有哪些运动？

观看视频 WATCHING THE VIDEO

同学 A 和同学 B 准备去上体育课了，让我们一起去看看他们的体育课是怎么样的吧！

扫描视频二维码观看

内容提示 CONTENT TIPS

Part 1

课文 text

有意思的体育课

同学A：这学期的体育课你选课了吗？

同学B：我选了太极课。

同学A：太极，听起来好有意思。

同学B：我也觉得，给你看看我们的上课视频。

同学A：哇，看起来好轻松。

同学B：才不是呢，太极的一招一式都有讲究，要练好可不容易。

同学A：原来如此。

同学B：那你选了什么课？

同学A：我选了安塞腰鼓课，全校就30个名额，别提多难抢了！

同学B：安塞腰鼓？那是什么？

同学A：安塞腰鼓是中国陕北的传统体育活动，我觉得还挺有意思的。

同学B：打鼓应该挺累的吧？

同学A：的确很累，但也很好玩儿！我觉得体育课是最有意思的课了。

同学B：我也喜欢上体育课。

生词 new words

体育 tǐyù [v.] physical education, sports

选课 xuǎnkè [v.] course selection

太极 tàijí [n.] Tai Chi

视频 shìpín [n.] video

轻松 qīngsōng [adj.] light, relaxed

一招一式 yīzhāo-yīshì [n.] every gesture and motion

讲究 jiǎngjiū [n.] careful study

原来如此 yuánlái-rúcǐ So that is what it is, I see

安塞腰鼓 ānsài yāogǔ [n.] Ansai waist drum

名额 míng'é [n.] the number of people assigned or allowed

抢 qiǎng [v.] snatch, grab

陕北 shǎnběi [n.] Northern Shaanxi

传统 chuántǒng [adj.] tradition, convention

打鼓 dǎ gǔ [v.] beat a drum

累 lèi [v.] tire out, wear out

的确 díquè [adv.] really, indeed

Part 2 注释 notes

1. 太极，听起来好有意思。

[形容词]“有意思”表示“有趣”，常用于口语中，可以在前面加上“很、好、挺、最”等表示程度的副词，其中“很有意思、好有意思、挺有意思”表示 "very interesting"，“最有意思”表示 "the most interesting"。例如：

[adj.]“有意思”means "interesting", which is often used in Spoken Chinese, and can be preceded by adverbs such as "very, good, quite, most" to indicate degree, where “很有意思、好有意思、挺有意思”means "very interesting", and“最有意思”means "the most interesting". For example:

① 我觉得学习汉语很有意思。

② 这本小说看起来好有意思。

③ 他说话还挺有意思的。

④ 我觉得打篮球最有意思。

2. 看起来好轻松。

“看起来”的意思是 "it seems or appears, it looks as if"。

“看起来” means "it seems or appears, it looks as if".

“起来”是趋向补语，跟在“看、听、说、吃”等单音节动词之后，后面可以接表示评价的短语或句子。“V+ 起来 + 评价”表示从某种角度对人或事物加以评价。例如：

“起来”can be used as a complement after a monosyllabic verb (e.g.“看、听、说、吃”) to express that the speaker has just initiated the action, and based on that, has made a preliminary judgement, in the form of a phrase or sentence that follows. “V+ 起来 + 评价”means to assess a person or a thing from a particular point of view. For example:

①他妈妈看起来很年轻。

②你的想法听起来不错。

③这道菜吃起来一般。

④这件事说起来好笑。

3. 才不是呢……

[副词]“才”表示强调。“才不是呢”表示“不是”。例如：

[adv.]“才”is used to emphasize.“才不是呢”means "no, not". For example:

① A：他是你同学吗？

B：他才不是我同学，他是我的老师。

② A：你汉语说得很好。
B：我的汉语一般，马克的汉语才好呢。
③ 今天放假，才不用上课呢。

4. 一招一式

在中国传统武术中，一招是一个或几个动作的组成，一式是某一个动作。

In traditional Chinese martial arts, a move consists of one or several actions, while a gesture refers to a specific action.

5. 要练好可不容易。

[副词]“可”表示强调，还可以用在问句里加强语气。例如：

[adv.] “可” is used for emphasis. When used in a rhetorical question, it strengthens the tone. For example:

① 今天你可不能迟到。
② 我可不认识他。
③ 图书馆今天不开门，这可怎么办？

6. 原来如此。

成语。“原来如此”表示“发现真实情况”“原来是这样”。

Idiom. “原来如此” means "discovering the truth" "finding out things being how it is".

7. 别提多难抢了！

You can't imagine how hard it is to get enrolled!

① 丽丽今天考了一百分，别提多高兴了！
② 食堂的菜别提多好吃了！
③ 这部电影别提多好看了！

8. 的确很累……

[副词]确实。“的确”表示对事实十分肯定。用在动词或形容词前，也可单独用在句子前面。例如：

[adv.] It means for sure, which means that one is quite certain of a fact. It is used before a verb or an adjective. It can also be used independently before a sentence. For example:

① 北京的确是一座美丽的城市。
② 迈克的确是美国人。
③ 珍妮的确很漂亮。

综合练习 COMPREHENSIVE PRACTICE

Part 1 视频练习

看视频，将句子和说话人的语气连线
Connect the following sentences with the speaker's tone

1. 太极，听起来好有意思。
2. 要练好可不容易。
3. 别提多难抢了！
4. 原来如此。
5. 打鼓应该挺累的吧？

A. 明白
B. 猜测
C. 强调
D. 感叹
E. 兴奋

看视频，选择填空 Watch the video and choose the best answer

1. 同学 A、B 分别选了什么体育课？ (　　)
   A. 太极；乒乓球
   B. 太极；安塞腰鼓
   C. 安塞腰鼓；太极
2. 太极课是什么样的体育课？ (　　)
   A. 看起来好轻松，要练好也很容易。
   B. 听起来很有意思，但一招一式都有讲究，要练好可不容易。
   C. 看起来挺有意思的，练起来很累，但也很好玩儿。
3. 安塞腰鼓这门体育课________，因为________。 (　　)
   A. 非常难抢；全校就 30 个名额
   B. 很难抢；每个年级就 30 个名额
   C. 一点也不难抢；全校有 300 个名额
4. 同学 A 觉得体育课是________的课。 (　　)
   A. 好有意思
   B. 挺有意思
   C. 最有意思

看视频，回答问题 Watch the video and answer the questions

1. 视频中，同学 A 对太极课的看法有哪些变化？
2. 结合视频，介绍一下安塞腰鼓这门体育课。
3. 视频里出现了哪些体育活动，你觉得哪种运动最有意思？

Part 2　书面练习

选词填空　Choose a word to fill in each blank

讲究　名额　传统　轻松　选课　体育　有意思

1. A：我们学校下午一点开始在网站上________，你准备好了吗？
   B：准备好了，我一定能抢到我喜欢的课。
2. 这次参加省篮球比赛的________很少，我们一定要加油！
3. A：我很喜欢上________课，我觉得它是最________的课。
   B：我才不喜欢呢，每次上课都很累。
4. 在篮球比赛中，我们班赢得很________。
5. A：我周末要和同学聚餐，你有什么推荐的吗？
   B：你可以去问问杰克，他在吃的方面很________。
6. 京剧是中国________的文化艺术。

完成句子　Complete the sentences

1. A：杰克会说汉语吗？
   B：当然啦，他____________。（可）
2. A：安娜，听说你一毕业就要结婚，这是真的吗？
   B：____________。（才）
3. A：看，这是我买的新衣服，怎么样？
   B：____________。（V+起来）
4. 这几天____________，你应该多穿一点。（挺）
5. 我不是不想参加同学聚会，____________。（的确）

句子配对　Match the sentences

1. 原来如此，	A. 她看起来很年轻。
2. 看到女儿考上医学院，	B. 现在我明白你的意思了。
3. 我喜欢杰夫的方案，	C. 我看啦，云南的确很美。
4. 我经常来这家店买衣服，	D. 我别提多高兴了！
5. 我看见安娜的妈妈在逛街，	E. 他的想法听起来最有意思。
6. 我去云南拍的照片你看了吗？	F. 这儿的东西挺好的。

Part 3 拓展练习

双人活动 Pair work

两人一组，互相说一说你们的周末计划，一人说计划，一人用“V +起来”进行评价。

提示词：看、听、说、吃、穿、做……

例如：

A：周末去图书馆怎么样？

B：听起来有点儿无聊。我们还是去逛商场吧！

A：好呀，去商场听起来还不错。

……

复述课文 Repeat the text

同学A：这学期的……你……了吗？

同学B：我选了……课。

同学A：……，听起来……。

同学B：我也觉得，给你看看我们的……。

同学A：哇，看起来……。

同学B：……，太极的……都有……，要练好……。

同学A：……。

同学B：那你选了什么课？

同学A：我选了……课，全校就……，别提多……了！

同学B：……？这是什么？

同学A：……是中国……的……体育活动，我觉得还……。

同学B：……应该挺……的吧？

同学A：……很累，但也……！我觉得……是……的课了。

同学B：我也喜欢上……。

口语表达 Oral expression

向同学们介绍一下自己最喜欢的体育运动，并说一说你为什么喜欢它。

例如：

我最喜欢的体育运动是打篮球。打篮球主要是跑步和投篮，看起来很简单，但其实不容易。因为它不是一项个人运动，而是一项团队运动。我觉得打篮球很有意思，因为不仅能锻炼身体，还能交到很多朋友……

文化链接 CULTURAL LINK

1. 太极 Taiji

太极即太极拳，是一种拳术运动，2020 年 12 月被联合国收入世界非物质文化遗产代表作名录。因为太极拳法变化多端，人们就用“太极”这一个哲学理论的名字来命名。此外，太极的许多招式还结合了易学（yìxué，一门哲学学问）的基础理论。太极流派很多，如陈氏、杨氏、武氏太极等。长期打太极拳，能够增强身体素质，还可以促进心理健康。这项传统运动目前仍然十分流行。在公园的一角，我们经常可以遇到一些中老年人，身穿传统中国服饰，在一起练习太极。他们热爱这一运动，并愿意将这个运动传承下去。

Taiji, or Taijiquan, is a boxing sport that was inscribed on the United Nations Representative List of the World Intangible Cultural Heritage in December 2020. It is named after the philosophical theory "Taiji" because of its many variations. In addition, many of the Taiji stances incorporate the underlying theory of "yìxué" (a philosophical discipline). There are many schools of Taiji, such as the Chen, Yang and Wu Taiji. Doing Taijiquan over a long period of time can enhance physical fitness and also promote mental health. This traditional exercise is still very popular. In one corner of the park, we can often meet some elderly and middle-aged people, dressed in traditional Chinese costumes, practising Taiji together. They love this sport and are willing to pass it on.

2. 安塞腰鼓 Ansai waist drum

安塞腰鼓最初是一种流传于陕西省延安市安塞区的传统舞蹈，也是中国的非物质文化遗产之一。安塞腰鼓的表演，较为自由、灵活。表演者人数可多可少，少则几人，多则上千人。

根据传说记载，黄帝和蚩尤（Chī Yóu，人名）的战争中，鼓是一种增加战斗气势的工具，为了便于携带，人们按照大鼓的样式做出了能够挂在腰间的小鼓。到了秦代，安塞地区一带战争较多，鼓成为重要的军事装备，一方面，可以利用鼓声传递情报，另一方面，人们在战争胜利后会用鼓声表示庆祝，但随着历史的发展，安塞腰鼓逐渐成为娱乐、伴奏的乐器。今天，安塞腰鼓仍然是一种值得欣赏的艺术形式。

The Ansai Waist Drum is a traditional dance originally passed down in the Ansei district of Yan'an, Shaanxi province, and is one of Chinese intangible cultural heritage. The performance of the Ansai Waist Drum is more free and flexible. The number of performers can be as small or as large as a few, or as many as a thousand.

According to legend, during the war between the Yellow Emperor and ChiYou (Chī Yóu, the name of the person), drums were a tool to increase the momentum of the battle, and in order to make them easier to carry, people made small drums that could be hung around the waist, following the style of the large drums. By the Qin Dynasty, when there were more wars around the Ansai region, the drums became important military equipment, on the one hand allowing the sound of the drums to be used to transmit information, and on the other hand, people would celebrate with the sound of the drums after a victory in war, but as history developed, the Ansai Waist Drum gradually became an instrument for entertainment and accompaniment. Today, the Ansai Waist Drum is still an art form to be appreciated.

6 气象小主播：芒种
Weather anchor: Grain in Ear

热身 WARMING UP

6 月，中国的夏天到了，你们国家这个时候是什么季节呢？天气怎么样？

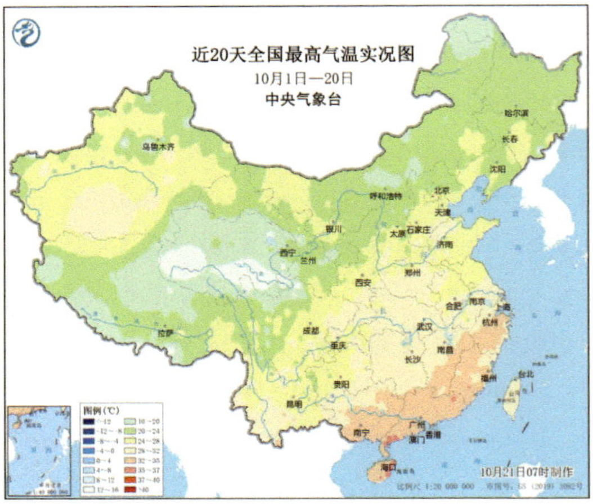

（图片来源：中央气象台官网）

观看视频 WATCHING THE VIDEO

中国夏天的天气怎么样呢？让气象小主播为我们播报最近的天气预告吧！

扫描视频二维码观看

内容提示 CONTENT TIPS

Part 1

课文 text

气象小主播：芒种

大家好！我是气象小主播张文杉，今天由我为大家说天气。

水国芒种后，梅天风雨凉。时间飞快，小满之后紧接着是芒种，以及一年一度的高考。芒种以及之后几天，将会一直持续多云，温度为27~32℃，体感温度较热。

高考安排在芒种期间并非巧合，因为这段时间是我国夏季气候条件最好的时候，也有利于高考的组织和考试工作，以及各大高校的招生、录取工作。

作为最独特的二十四节气，芒种与高考密不可分，包含“一收一种”的含义，就像高考，有付出才有回报，有播种方有收获。

本期天气预报就到这里，我们下期再见。

生词 new words

芒种 mángzhòng [n.] Grain in Ear. It is a Mount crops such as wheat mature meaning.

小满 xiǎomǎn [n.] Grain buds. It means the seeds of summer crops begin to be plump.

高考 gāokǎo [n.] college entrance examination

持续 chíxù [v.] continue

多云 duōyún [n.] cloudy

体感温度 tǐgǎn wēndù [n.] sensible temperature

安排 ānpái [v.] arrange

巧合 qiǎohé [n.] coincidence

气候 qìhòu [n.] climate

组织 zǔzhī [v.] organize

招生 zhāoshēng [v.] enroll new students

录取 lùqǔ [v.] enroll

独特 dútè [adj.] unique

二十四节气 èrshísì jiéqì the 24 solar terms

天气预报 tiānqì yùbào weather forecast

Part 2 注释 notes

1. 由

[介词] 用于引入动作的施动者。例如：

[prep.] By “由” introduces the agent of an action. For example:

① 班长由安娜担任。
② 这次晚会由杰克主持。
③ 今天的作业由老师布置。

2. 以及

[连词] 用来连接并列关系的词或词组，连接成分一般有主次或先后的分别。例如：

[Conjunction] "以及" is used to connect words or phrases that have a coordinate relationship, with the connected components generally differ in priority or sequence. For example:

① 我喜欢打篮球、踢足球以及跑步。
② 他去过北京以及上海。
③ 在学习以及工作中，我们都要有认真的态度。

3. 一年一度

成语。意思是每年一次。

An idiom that means "once a year" or "annually".

① 明天就是学校一年一度的美食节。
② 一年一度的暑假马上开始了。

4. 将

[副词] 用于书面。可以表示动作或情况不久就要发生。例如：

[adv.] Be going to "将" is used in written Chinese, meaning an action or situation is going to take place soon. For example:

① 火车将要出发了。
② 玛丽将去中国学习一年。

也可以表示对未来情况的判断，含有"肯定、一定"的意思。例如：

It may also be a judgement to the future situation, meaning "affirmation and certain". For example:

① 如果不努力学习，他将不能通过 HSK 考试。
② 我们将永远记住在中国的留学生活。

5. 并非

[副词] 表示"并不是"的意思。加强否定的语气。一般在不同意对方的说法、反驳对方时使用。后面常和"只是""而是""是"等连用。可用于句首。例如：

[adv] Actually not "并非" emphasizes the negative tone, usually it is used to disagree one's opinion or to argue other's point of view. It is usually used together with "只是" "而是" and "是" after it, and it can be used at the beginning of a sentence. For example:

① 我并非不想去学校，只是最近生病了。

② 并非每个人都喜欢吃火锅。

6. 密不可分

成语。形容十分紧密，不能分割。例如：

Idiom.It is used to describe something as very tight-knit and inseparable. For example:

① 成功和努力密不可分。

② 我和乔治是密不可分的好朋友。

7. 一收一种

指芒种时节，有芒的作物应收割，谷物作物应播种。

An idiom that refers to the Grain in Ear season, when crops with awns should be harvested, and grain crops should be planted.

8. 就

[副词] 常表示强调、肯定的语气，意思是"是这个，不是别的"。例如：

[adv.] The word "就" implies the mood of emphasis and affirmative. It is this one, not others. For example:

① 我们的汉语老师就是王老师。

② 她就像我的妹妹一样可爱。

综合练习　COMPREHENSIVE PRACTICE

Part 1　视频练习

看视频，判断对错　Watch the video and judge true or false

1. 小满在芒种之后。　（　）
2. 高考一年举办一次。　（　）
3. 芒种之后的天气较热。　（　）
4. 高考安排在芒种期间是巧合。　（　）
5. 芒种的含义就像高考一样有付出才有收获。　（　）

看视频，选择填空　Watching video and choose the best answer

1. “水国芒种后，梅天风雨凉。”是指哪个节气？　(　　)

A. 小满　　B. 梅天　　C. 芒种

2. 芒种期间的天气是什么？　(　　)

A. 偶尔多云　　B. 持续多云　　C. 持续少云

3. 芒种以及之后几天的温度可能是多少度？　(　　)

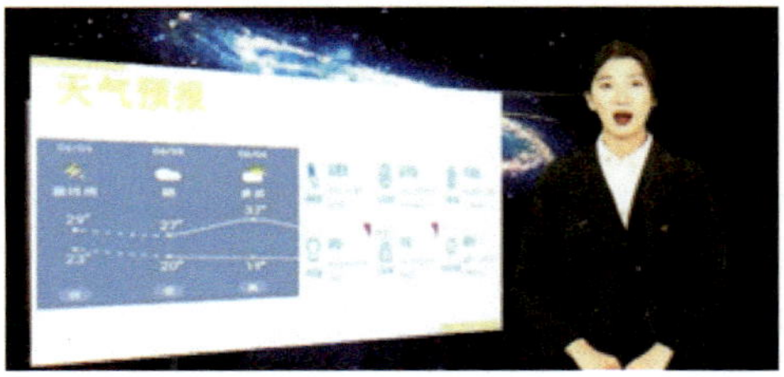

A.25℃　　B.28℃　　C.33℃

4. 芒种之后的体感温度是什么？　(　　)

A. 较热　　B. 很热　　C. 不热

看视频，回答问题　Watch the video and answer the questions

1. 本期天气预报主要介绍了什么？
2. 为什么高考会安排在芒种期间？
3. 为什么说“芒种与高考密不可分”？

Part 2　书面练习

选词填空　Choose a word to fill in each blank

密不可分　　巧合　　独特　　持续　　组织　　一年一度

1. A：我发现我们的生日是同一天！
   B：这可真是个________。
2. 这场大雨________下了三天。
3. A：你觉得小美和这件事有关系吗？
   B：我认为她和这件事的关系________。
4. 为了迎接________的运动会，我们学校今天放假。
5. 明天我要参加学校________的交流会。
6. 他的学习方法很________。

完成句子　Complete sentences

1. A：你学习汉语的方法有哪些？
   B：________________________________（以及）
2. 明天的生日会____________________________（由）
3. A：你觉得送礼物是不是越贵越好？
   B：________________________________（并非）
4. A：暑假你要做什么？
   B：________________________________（将）

连词成句　Match the words into a sentence

1. 就　　前面　　图书馆　　是

____

2. 教室　　就　　我　　坐在

____

3. 有　　努力　　就　　收获

____

4. 写作业　　我　　不　　就

____

Part 3　拓展练习

你问我答　Ask and answer

两人一组，一人提问，一人回答。问题：今天的天气怎么样？适合去做什么？

提示词：晴天、雨天、阴天、太阳、下雨、多云、冷、热……

例如：

A：今天的天气怎么样？

B：今天是晴天，天气很好，但是有点热。

A：今天可以去做什么呢？

B：我们可以去野餐。

复述课文　Repeat the text

大家好！我是……张文杉，今天……为大家说天气。

水国芒种后，梅天风雨凉。时间飞快，……之后紧接着是……，以及……的高考。芒种……之后几天，……一直……，……为 27~32℃，……较热。同学们应做好……，避免……。

高考……在……并非……，因为这段时间是我国……最好的时候，也有利于高考的……工作，以及各大高校的……工作。

作为最独特的……，芒种与高考……，包含“……”的含义，……高考，有……才有……，有……方有……。

本期……就到这里，我们……。

角色扮演　Role-play

如果你是“气象小主播”，请你查找某天的天气情况，并为大家进行播报。

例如：

大家好！我是气象小主播玛丽，今天由我为大家说天气。

今天是 2022 年 7 月 18 日，星期一，今天的温度为 26~33℃，体感温度较热，天气阴转多云。同学们要注意……

本期天气预报就到这里，我们下期再见。

文化链接 CULTURAL LINK

1. 中国古诗与二十四节气 Ancient Chinese poetry and the 24 solar terms

“水国芒种后，梅天风雨凉”这句诗出自唐代诗人窦常的《北固晚眺》。意思是：长江、淮河地区自芒种时节后，梅雨即将到来，天气慢慢变得凉快。诗句含义简单，但却能表现出诗人对于生活的认真观察和思考。二十四节气是中国传统农历中特有的现象。诗人们在自然的风、雨、霜、雪等节气天气的变化中得到启发，创作了许多与节气相关的经典作品。中国古诗与二十四节气的密切关系，也反映了中国“天人合一”的传统文化思想。

This poem is from the poet Dou Chang of the Tang Dynasty, who wrote "A view of the evening in Beigu". The poem means that the weather in the Yangtze and Huai River regions is slowly becoming cooler as the plum rains are about to arrive after the mango seeding season. The meaning of the verse is simple, but it shows the poet's careful observation and reflection on life. The 24 solar terms are a phenomenon unique to the traditional Chinese lunar calendar. Poets have been inspired by the natural changes of wind, rain, frost and snow in the festivals and have composed many classical works related to the festivals. The close relationship between ancient Chinese poetry and the 24 solar terms also reflects the traditional Chinese cultural idea of "the unity of heaven and man".

（陈凯雯 摄）

2. “金榜题名”成语故事 Idiom story: "One's name was put on the published list of successful candidates"

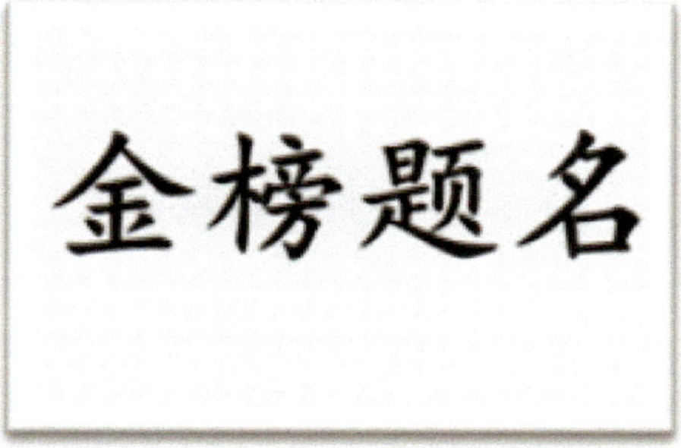

传说一个名叫崔绍的人，在病中做了一个梦，梦到他来到阴间（yīnjiān，传说中人类死亡后，其灵魂所在的地方），发现在阴间里写着人名的榜单由不同的材料组成，分为金榜、银榜和铁榜。在金榜上的人物都是重要官员；银榜上的人物则是身份、地位次要一些的；而

地方上的官员名字被写在铁榜上。由于这个传说，后来人们一般认为，金榜象征着重要的地位和高等的官职，金榜题名的意思是得到较高的社会地位或成为重要官员。而现在，祝福对方考试顺利的意思则更加流行、通用。

Legend has it that a man named CuiShao had a dream while he was sick that he came to the netherworld (yīnjiān, the place where the souls of human beings are located after death) and found that the lists of names written in the netherworld were made up of different materials, divided into gold, silver and iron lists. The figures on the Golden List were important officials; those on the Silver List were of lesser status and position; and the names of local officials were written on the Iron List. As a result of this legend, it was later generally believed that the Golden List symbolized important status and higher official positions, and that the Golden List meant getting a higher social status or becoming an important official. Nowadays, on the other hand, the meaning of wishing each other success in examinations is more popular and universal.

3. 高考　Gaokao

中国普通高等学校招生采取全国统一考试，简称高考。这是一项全国范围内人才选拔考试，考生主要为高中三年级的学生。这场考试的成绩将成为大学录取的依据，因此，这也是一场中国学生成长过程中相当重要的考试。考试的时间大体上是每年的 6 月 7—8 日 (部分地区为 3 天)。高考已经经历了多次改革，在不同的省（区、市），高考会推出不同的方案。高考的主要科目是语文、数学和英语，除此之外，考生可以根据自己的意愿，选择不同的学习方向，并参加其他不同科目的考试。

The National Unified Examination for Admission to Universities in China, or Gaokao for short. This is a nationwide talent selection examination, and the candidates are mainly students in their third year of high school. The results of this examination are used as the basis for admission to universities, making it a very important examination in the development of Chinese students. The exams are held roughly on 7-8 June each year (or 3 days in some areas). The Gaokao exam has undergone several reforms and different schemes are introduced in different provinces and cities. The main subjects in the exam are language, mathematics and English. In addition to these, candidates can choose different study directions and take examinations in other different subjects, depending on their wishes.

7 我的室友是网络作家
My roommate is an internet writer

热身 WARMING UP

现在，我们的生活离不开互联网。我们可以利用互联网学习，可以在网上购物，可以在网上支付……你会用互联网做什么呢？

上网课　　网上购物　　网上支付

观看视频 WATCHING THE VIDEO

有一个同学最近正在网络上看小说，我们一起看看发生了什么吧？

扫描视频二维码观看

内容提示　CONTENT TIPS

Part 1

课文　text	生词　new words

我的舍友是网络作家

（同学 B 在写小说，电脑屏幕显示"修改成功"）

同学A：啊！终于更新了！

同学B：什么更新了？

同学A：是我之前看的一部小说，已经很久没有出过新内容了。我以为作者已经半途而废了，没想到今天他又更新了。

同学B：哦~

（B 的电脑屏幕显示"发表成功"）

作家 zuòjiā [n.] author, writer

屏幕 píngmù [n.] screen

修改 xiūgǎi [v.] revise, amend

终于 zhōngyú [adv.] at last, in the end, finally, eventually

更新 gēngxīn [v.] update

小说 xiǎoshuō [n.] novel, fiction

内容 nèiróng [n.] content

作者 zuòzhě [n.] author, writer

半途而废 bàntú–érfèi give up halfway, do a thing by halves

发表 fābiǎo [v.] publish

Part 2　注释　notes

1. 终于

[副词] 表示经过较长的过程之后最后出现的结果。多用于希望达到的结果。例如：

[adv.] It means a result comes into being after a long process. Usually, it implies an expected result. For example:

① 在学校五个月了，现在终于放假了。

② 我等了他两个小时，他终于来了。

③ 我们走了好久，终于到公园了。

2. 已经

[副词] 表示动作完成或者达到某种程度。例如：

[adv.] It indicates that an action has been completed or having reached a certain degree. For example:

① 我已经到家了。

② 她学汉语已经三年了。

③ 弟弟已经十岁了。

3. ……已经很久没有出过新内容了。

"V+ 过"表示动作或状态在过去已经发生。例如：

"V+ 过" means an action or a state happened already in the past. For example:

S	V	过	O	了
他	吃	过	早餐	了
我们	读	过	课文	了
杰克	写	过	作业	了

"V+ 过"还可以用来强调过去有某种经历。例如：

"V+ 过" is used to emphasize a past experience. For example:

S	V	过	O
他	当	过	英语老师
我	去	过	北京
乔治	吃	过	法国菜

否定形式是在动词前边加"没（有）"。例如：

The negative form is made by adding "没 (有)" before the verb. For example:

S	没（有）+V	过	O
他	没学	过	日语
我	没去	过	上海
乔治	没有吃	过	饺子

4. 我以为作者已经半途而废了，没想到今天他又更新了。

"以为"用来表达此前不符合客观事实的想法，"没想到"用来表达说话人意识到了一个意想不到的事实。"以为"后面常常会再带"没想到、结果、其实、谁知道、原来"引导的小句，说明事实情况。例如：

"以为" "mistakenly think that", is the same as "thought" in English when we talk about mistaken beliefs. "没想到" indicates that the speaker has realized an unexpected fact. The clause that follows "以为" is the mistaken belief or incorrect information. A second sentence often follows to show the true information, starting with "没想到、结果、其实、谁知道、原来". For example:

① 今天是周六，我以为不上课，没想到要补课。

② A：你写完作业了吗？

B：还没有，我以为作业很简单，没想到这么难。

③ 玛丽生病了，我以为她会请假，没想到她坚持来上课。

5. 半途而废

成语。意思是半路上就停下来了，比喻做事不能坚持。例如：

Idiom. It means to stop on the way. Analogy of doing things without sticking to the end. For example:

① 还没到终点，他就半途而废了。

② 你不要半途而废，作业还差一点点就写完了。

综合练习 COMPREHENSIVE PRACTICE

Part 1 视频练习

看视频，将句子和说话人的语气连线
Connect the following sentences with the speaker's tone

1. 终于更新了。	A. 惊喜
2. 我以为作者已经半途而废了……	B. 高兴
3. 什么更新了？	C. 难过
4. 没想到今天他又更新了。	D. 疑问

看视频，选择填空 Watch the video and choose the best answer

1. 同学 A 进宿舍的时候，同学 B 在做什么？ （ ）

A. 打游戏　　B. 看视频　　C. 写小说

2. 同学 A 发现了什么？（ ）

A. 老师布置作业了　　B. 游戏更新了　　C. 小说更新了

3. 发现更新后，同学 A 感觉怎么样？（ ）

A. 伤心　　B. 惊喜　　C. 失望

4. 同学 B “发表成功”，发表的是什么？（ ）

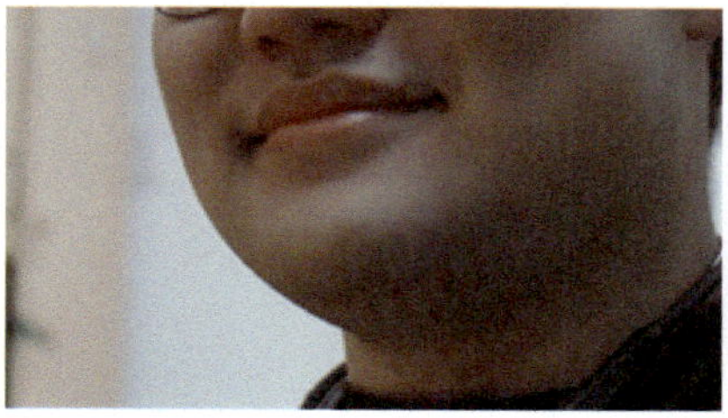

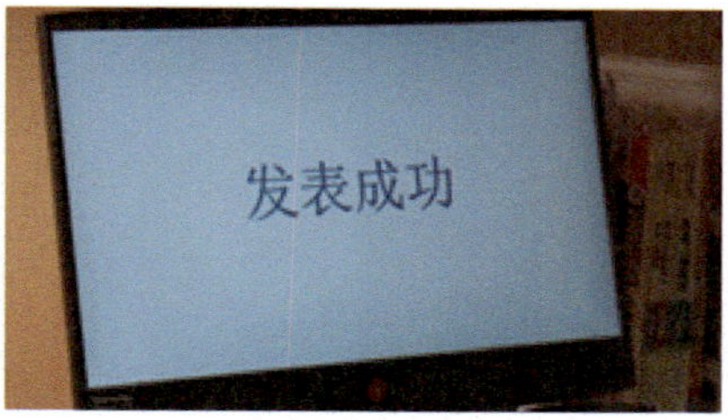

A. 小说　　B. 论文　　C. 朋友圈

看视频，回答问题　Watch the video and answer the questions

1. 你知道谁是小说的作者吗？同学 A 知道吗？
2. 同学 B 为什么笑了？

Part 2　书面练习

选词填空　Choose a word to fill in each blank

更新　　没想到　　终于　　内容　　小说　　修改

1. 我很喜欢这篇文章的________。

2. 你的作业里有很多错误，需要回去________。
3. 王明很喜欢看________，吃饭看，走路也看。
4. 我最近在看一部很好看的电视剧，它每周六________一集。
5. 坐了二十个小时的火车，我________到北京了。
6. 平时我们的作业很多，________今天没有作业。

完成句子　Complete the sentences

1. A：这座山太高了，我不想爬了。
   B：再坚持一会儿，我们已经爬到一半了，________。（半途而废）
2. 我来中国________了。（已经）
3. A：你怎么带伞了？
   B：我________，________。（以为……没想到……）
4. 我减肥一年了，现在________。（终于）

句子配对　Match the sentences

1. 我以为她是爱我的，　　A. 没想到突然下大雨了。
2. 丽丽以为她会迟到，　　B. 没想到她骗了我。
3. 杰瑞以为今天可以出去玩，　　C. 没想到他一直没有来。
4. 他以为这次比赛自己会输，　　D. 没想到她很早就到教室了。
5. 我们以为他会来参加聚会，　　E. 没想到居然得了第一名。
6. 大家以为老师去北京了，　　F. 没想到还是赶上了火车。

Part 3　拓展练习

口语表达　Oral expression

1. 你看过中国小说吗？是什么小说？
2. 你看过中国电影吗？是什么电影？
3. 你吃过中国菜吗？是什么菜？
4. 你去旅游过吗？去过哪里？

复述课文　Repeat the text

同学A推开门走进……，这时同学B在……上写……。
同学A坐下后……地说："啊！终于……！"
同学B问："什么……？"
同学A回答："是我之前看的……，已经很久……了。我以为作者……，没想到……。”

同学B说：“……”，然后他……。

最后，同学B的电脑显示“……成功”。

角色扮演 Role-play

两人一组，一人扮演A，一人扮演B。结束后请两组同学上台表演。

A：你是马克的朋友，今天马克生病了，你去他家看望他，你会对他说什么呢？	B：你是马克，朋友来看望生病的你，你会怎么回答朋友的问候？

提示词：测体温、去医院、看医生、吃药、打针……

要求：用“……过……”提问与回答。

文化链接 CULTURAL LINK

1. “半途而废”成语故事 Idiom Story: “Doing A Thing by Halves”

战国时期，有一个叫乐羊子的人，离开家到很远的地方去拜师学艺。一天，他的妻子正在家里织布，乐羊子突然回来了。

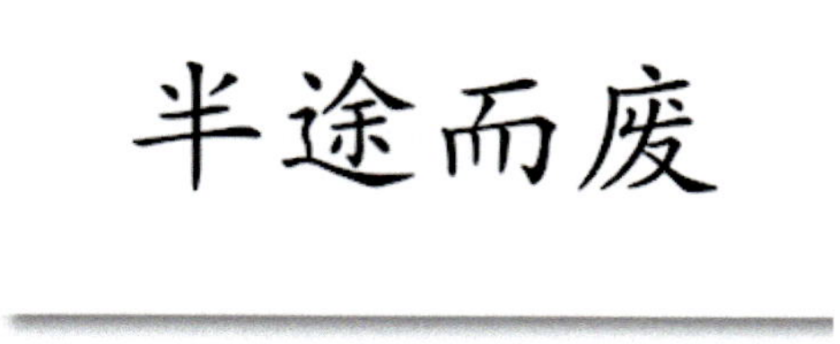

他的妻子觉得奇怪，便问：“你怎么这么快就学完了？”乐羊子说：“没有，我在外面想家了，所以回来看看你。”他的妻子听了以后，拿起剪刀把一块已经织好的布剪成两段，然后对他说：“这布是我辛辛苦苦、一点一点织出来的，现在我把它剪断了，就等于以前的时间和辛苦都白费了。你拜师求学，和我纺线织布是一样的！半路上放弃了，以前付出的努力也白费了。”于是乐羊子离开家，继续去学习了。

During the Warring States Period, there was a man named Le Yangzi who left home to go far away to apprenticeship. One day, his wife was weaving at home, and Le Yangzi suddenly came back.

His wife felt strange, so she asked: "Why did you finish your studies so soon?" Le Yangzi said: "No, I missed home outside, so I came back to see you." After his wife heard this, she took up scissors and cut a piece of cloth that had been woven into two pieces, and then said to him: "I knit this cloth bit by bit, and now I cut it. It means that the previous time and hard work have been wasted. You go to study with a teacher, spinning and weaving are the same as me! Give up halfway, and the previous efforts have been wasted." So Le Yangzi left home and continued to study.

2. 中国网络小说　Chinese Net Fiction

中国网络小说起步较晚，第一批写手主要是海外留学生。前期处于自由发展阶段，基本延续了传统文学写作的思路，随后逐步建立了自己的商业模式，并走向了以类型小说创作为主的发展阶段。由于移动阅读的普及，网络文学写作和阅读群体迅速扩大，人人都可以参与，成为大众文化的重要组成部分。尤其是网络小说数量众多，以此衍生出绘画、动漫、影视、游戏等系列文化作品。

今天，由网络小说改编的影视剧种类多样，市场效益好、收入高，在影视行业里比重逐渐加大，又反向推动了网络小说的高点击率和文本阅读率。

Chinese net fictions started late, and the first batch of writers were mainly overseas students. In the early stage of free development, it continued the idea of traditional literary writing, and then gradually established its own business model and moved to a development stage dominated by genre novels. Due to the popularity of mobile reading, net literature writing and reading groups have expanded rapidly, and everyone can participate. Net fictions become an important part of popular culture. In particular, there are a large number of online novels, from which a series of cultural works such as painting, animation, film and television, and games are derived.

Today, there are various types of film and television dramas adapted from online novels, and the market benefits and income are high, and their proportion in the film and television industry has increased, which in turn promotes the high click-through rate and text reading rate of online novels.

8 作业风波：“借鉴”
Assignment disturbance：use for reference

热身 WARMING UP

同学们，你们的作业都能按时完成吗？如果老师布置的作业你们不会做或者来不及完成了，你们会怎么办呢？

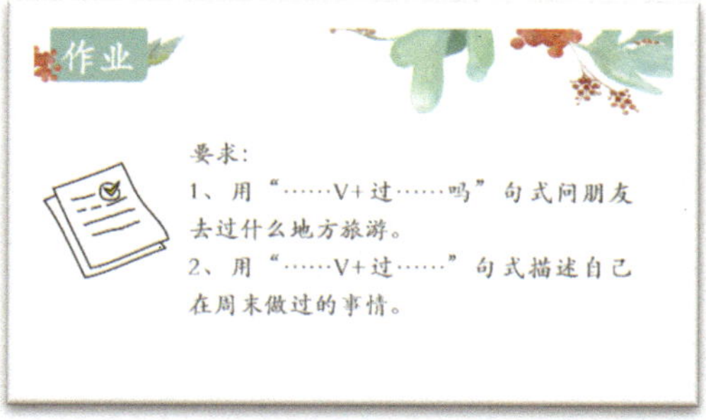

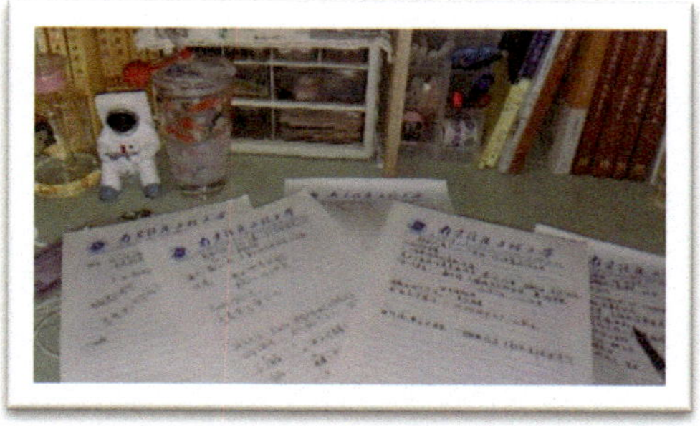

观看视频 WATCHING THE VIDEO

宿舍里的两位同学都在写作业，同学 A 已经写完了，但是同学 B 来不及写了，那他会怎么做呢？

扫描视频二维码观看

内容提示　CONTENT TIPS

Part 1

课文　text	生词　new words

作业风波："借鉴"

（同学 A 边整理作品集边敲门）

同学B：来了……看啥呢？

同学A：我正在整理作品。

同学B：这么多，你没少画吧。

同学A：还好还好，就这样吧。

同学B：你已经获了那么多奖了，你就满足吧！

（同学 A 接到外卖员电话）

同学A：喂，你好。好的，我现在就去拿。

（同学 A 走后）

同学B：我记得密码是……也就一般吧，没什么特殊的。他怎么这么容易获奖呢？这张好像还不错……

（同学 B 拿出手机拍下同学 A 的作品）

（几天后）

同学B：截止时间是——明天！借鉴借鉴，不算抄袭。

（同学 B 拿出手机画同学 A 的作品）

（两天后，刘老师打分，同学 B 的作

风波 fēngbō [n.] disturbance

借鉴 jièjiàn [v.] use for reference, draw lessons from

作品集 zuòpǐnjí [n.] collection

整理 zhěnglǐ [v.] arrange, put in order

满足 mǎnzú [v.] satisfied, content

外卖员 wàimàiyuán [n.] take out clerk

密码 mìmǎ [n.] secret code, password

一般 yībān [adj.] general, common

特殊 tèshū [adj.] special, particular

容易 róngyì [adj.] easy, ready

获奖 huòjiǎng [n.] win a prize

截止时间 jiézhǐ shíjiān [n.] deadline

抄袭 chāoxí [n.] plagiarize, copy

打分 dǎfēn [v.] grade, score

业98分）

同学A：你抄袭了我的画！

同学B：我……我那只是借鉴……

同学A：借鉴了百分之九十？你这是侵犯了我的知识产权啊！我的这些作品是要发表的，你先投稿了我还怎么发表？

同学B：对不起……

同学A：我们去找刘老师，这件事我需要维护我的正当权益。

（刘老师把同学B的98分改成了0分）

侵犯 qīnfàn [v.] infringe upon

知识产权 zhīshi chǎnquán [n.] intellectual property right

发表 fābiǎo [v.] publish

投稿 tóugǎo [v.] contribute, submit sth. for publication

维护 wéi hù [v.] safeguard, defend

正当权益 zhèngdàng quányì [n.] legitimate rights and interests

Part 2 注释 notes

1. 看啥呢？

[疑问代词]"啥"表示"什么"，常用于口语中。例如：

[Interrogative pronoun] "啥" means '"what" and is often used in Spoken Chinese. For example:

① 看啥呢？ = 看什么呢？

② 你想吃啥？ = 你想吃什么？

③ 啥东西啊？ = 什么东西啊？

2. 还好还好

这里的重复表示强调和谦虚的含义，类似的表达还有"哪里哪里""没有没有"。例如：

Repetition here means emphasis and modesty, the similar expressions are "哪里哪里""没有没有". For example:

① A：你的汉语说得真好！

B：还好还好，我学汉语很久了。

② A：你好厉害啊，考了这么高的分数。

B：哪里哪里，大家都考得很好。

③ A：你长得真好看！

B：没有没有，你也很好看。

3. 你已经获了这么多奖了。

“获奖”是离合动词。离合动词是指一些动宾结构的双音节动词，如“睡觉、毕业、见面、聊天、游泳”等这样的词，它们既可以作为一个词单独使用，又可以分开使用，在中间加上其他词语，如“睡一觉、毕了业、见个面、聊会儿天、游个泳”。

Separable verbs refer to some verb-object disyllable verbs, such as “睡觉 (sleep), 毕业 (graduate), 见面 (meet), 聊天 (chat), 游泳 (swim) ” and so on. The two characters that form the word are normally combined together to express an integrated meaning. However, sometimes the word can be separated by inserting some other characters between the two characters, such as “睡一觉、毕了业、见个面、聊会儿天、游个泳” .

（1）它们在使用时大多数不能带宾语；带关涉对象时，一般要用介词引入，充当动词的状语。例如：

Normally, they cannot be followed by objects. If a concerned object follows the verb, usually a preposition is used to be the adverbial of the verb. For example:

① 我今年大学毕业了。　★我今年毕业了大学。（×）

② 丽娜和他见面了。　★丽娜见面他了。（×）

（2）离合动词中间可以插入其他成分。例如：

Other components can be inserted into the separable verbs. For example:

① 我睡了半天觉。

② 他们见了两次面。

（3）离合动词的重叠形式为“AAB”式。例如：

Gemination form of separable verbs is "AAB". For example:

见见面、聊聊天、游游泳。

4. 没什么特殊的。

“没什么 + Adj. + 的”句式用来强调否定语气，如“没什么特殊的” = “不特殊，一般”。例如：

The sentence pattern “没什么 + Adj. + 的” is used to emphasize a negative tone, such as “没什么特殊的” which means "not special, just ordinary". For example:

① 说汉语没什么难的。= 说汉语不难。说汉语很简单。

② 这件事没什么好笑的。= 这件事不好笑。

③ 这里没什么好玩儿的。= 这里不好玩儿。

5. 他怎么这么容易获奖呢？

[代词]“这么”是指示代词，用来指示程度。“这么 +Adj.”强调说话人的感叹

语气，意思是"非常、多么"。"这么"有略带夸张、使语言生动的作用。例如：

[pron.] "这么" is a demonstrative pronoun indicating degree. The structure "这么 + Adj." emphasizes the exclamation of the speaker, meaning "very, so much". The phrases "这么" has a slight exaggerated sense, but makes the speech vivid. For example:

① 我没想到他的汉语说得这么好。

② 你来中国已经这么久了啊。

6. 借鉴借鉴，不算抄袭。

动词的重叠形式用来表达短时间、少量、轻微、尝试的意思，语气比较轻松、随便，多用于口语中。

The reduplicative form of a verb indicates a short time, a small quantity, a slight degree or an attempt, conveying a relaxed and casual mood. It is often used in Spoken Chinese.

（1）单音动词的重叠形式：

Reduplicative forms of monosyllabic verbs:

A	AA	A一A
说	说说	说一说
看	看看	看一看
跑	跑跑	跑一跑

（2）双音节动词的重叠形式：

Reduplicative forms of disyllabic verbs:

AB	ABAB
学习	学习学习
讨论	讨论讨论
休息	休息休息

综合练习 COMPREHENSIVE PRACTICE

Part 1 视频练习

看视频，将句子和说话人的语气连线

Connect the following sentences with the speaker's tone

1. 这么多，你没少画。　　　　A. 生气（angry）

2. 还好还好，就这样吧。　　B. 羡慕（admire）
3. 他怎么这么容易获奖呢？　　C. 心虚（guilty）
4. 你先投稿了我还怎么发表？　　D. 嫉妒（envy）
5. 我……我那只是借鉴……　　E. 谦虚（modest）

看视频，选择填空 Watch the video and choose the best answer

1. 视频开头，同学 A 在做什么？（　　）

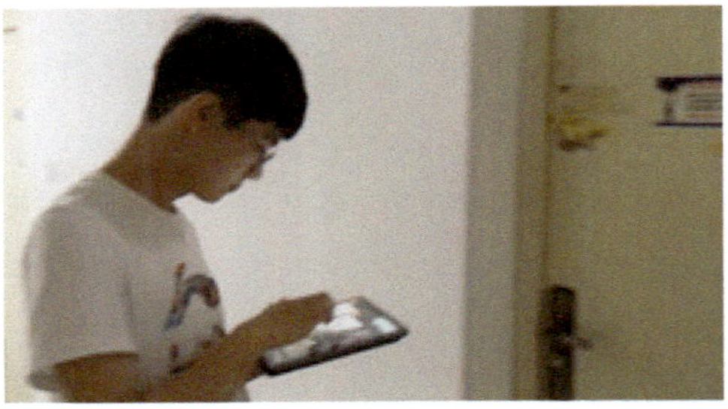

A. 看作业要求　　B. 整理作品集　　C. 点外卖　　D. 看小说

2. 同学 A 出门后，同学 B 做了什么？（　　）

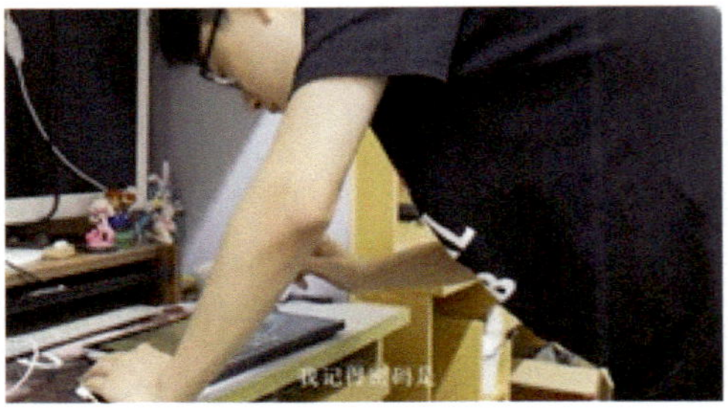

A. 欣赏并夸赞同学 A 的作品　　B. 用同学 A 的平板打游戏
C. 偷拍同学 A 的作品　　D. 偷偷修改同学 A 的作品

3. 同学 B 把作业交上去之后，同学 A 的作品会怎么样？（　　）

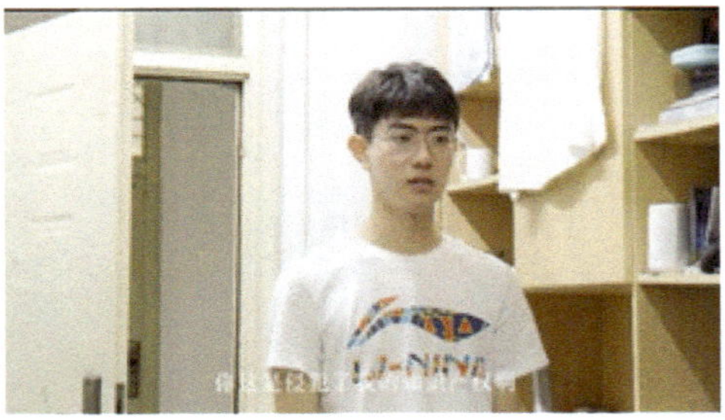

A. 不可以发表了　　B. 可以继续投稿
C. 很容易获奖　　D. 被认为很一般

4. 同学 B 的最终成绩是？　　　　　　　　　　　　　　　　　（　　）

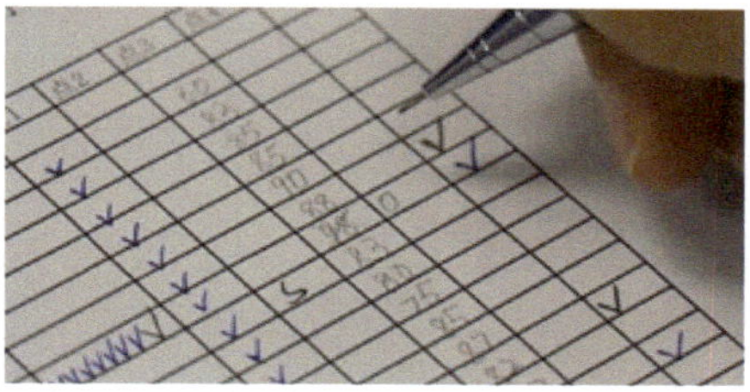

A. 98 分　　　B. 60 分　　　C. 0 分　　　D. 85 分

看视频，回答问题　Watch the video and answer the questions

1. 同学 B 认为同学 A 的作品怎么样？
2. 同学 A 最终是怎么样维护他的正当权益的？

Part 2　书面练习

选词填空　Choose a word to fill in each blank

整理　　满足　　投稿　　维护　　发表　　截止

1. A：我的目标是瘦到九十斤[①]。
   B：你都已经这么瘦了，怎么还不________？
2. 运动会报名的________日期是下周六。
3. 当我们的知识产权受到侵犯时，要勇敢________自己的正当权益。
4. A：安妮，恭喜你的论文________啦！
   B：谢谢。
5. 下午开会的资料是由我________的。
6. A：你今天怎么这么高兴呀？
   B：我________的作品获奖啦。

完成句子　Complete the sentences

1. A：________________________________？（啥）
   B：我想吃火锅。
2. A：下节课的道具你准备好了吗？
   B：当然啦，________________________。（容易）
3. 没想到今天的作业________________________。（这么）

① 1 斤 =0.5 千克。

4. A：这本书你看过吗？你觉得怎么样？
B：________________________________。（一般）
5. A：周末你在家里做什么？
B：________________________________。（动词重叠式）

句子配对 Match the sentences

1. 你在干啥呢？
2. 你写的字真好看！
3. 约翰和她什么时候见的面？
4. 去旅游感觉怎么样？
5. 你的汉语怎么说得这么好？
6. 好累啊，怎么还没到？

A. 好像是两天前。
B. 一般吧，那里没什么好玩儿的。
C. 我正在运动。
D. 因为我来中国已经三年了。
E. 那我们休息休息再走吧。
F. 还好还好，就那样吧。

Part 3 拓展练习

双人活动 Pair work

两人一组，每个人想两个能重叠的动词，并根据对方想出来的动词重叠式进行造句。

例如：

A：看 / 看看 / 看一看 → B：我想看看你的手机。
B：讨论 / 讨论讨论 → A：我们讨论讨论今天的作业。

A. 动词 1（________） → B：句子 1________________。
动词 2（________） → B：句子 2________________。
B. 动词 1（________） → A：句子 1________________。
动词 2（________） → A：句子 2________________。

复述课文 Repeat the text

同学 A 边……边……。

同学 B 开门后问他：“看……？”同学 A 回答：“我正在……。”同学 B 说：“……，你没少画吧。”同学 A 回答：“……，就这样吧。”同学 B 又说：“你已经……，你就……吧！”

这时，同学 A 接到……的电话，他说：“喂，……。好的，我现在……。”

同学 A 走后，同学 B 去看了他的平板电脑，同学 B 边看边说：“我记得……也就……吧，没什么……的。他怎么……获奖呢？这张好像……。”然后他拿出手机拍下同学A的……。

几天后，同学B发现……是明天，他来不及了，于是他……画……，他说："……，不算……。"

两天后，同学B的作业拿了……分。同学A很生气地说："你……我的画！"同学B说："我……我那只是……。"同学A问："……了百分之九十？你这是……了我的……啊！我的这些……是要……的，你先……我还怎么……？"同学B道歉："……"同学A说："我们去……，这件事我需要……我的……。"

最后，刘老师把同学B的分数改成了……分。

口语表达　Oral expression

1. 你认为同学B的做法是借鉴还是抄袭？为什么？你怎么看待这种行为？
2. 在同学们生活中你们知道哪些侵犯知识产权的行为吗？

例如：盗版电影（Pirated movies）

文化链接　CULTURAL LINK

1. 中国的知识产权发展史
The history of intellectual property in China

在春秋战国时期，人们为了表明自己的身份或所属的派别，就已经开始在作品上留下自己的名字。在唐朝时期，政府禁止人们不经过政府允许复印与国家历史、法律相关的重要书籍。到了宋代，活字印刷术的发明推动了版权制度的进程。私人印刷者需要将出版物送交政府部门，接受政府的审核和检查。出版物通过之后，才可以在书上印上"不许盗版"的字样，表示合法。宋代商业非常发达，还出现了商标。清政府开始建立近代相关的知识产权制度。目前，中国已经建立了比较完整的知识产权法律体系。

During the Spring and Autumn and Warring States periods, people began to put their names on their works in order to identify themselves or the faction to which they belonged. During the Tang Dynasty, the government forbade people from making copies of important books relating to the history and laws of the country without the government's permission. By the Song Dynasty, the invention of movable type gave impetus to the copyright system. Private printers were required to send their publications to government departments for review and inspection by the government. Only after the publication had been approved could the words "No piracy" be printed on the book to indicate that it was legal. During the Song Dynasty, commerce was very advanced and trademarks were introduced. The

Qing government began to establish a modern intellectual property system. China now has a relatively complete legal system for intellectual property.

2. 必出于己，不袭蹈前人一言一句。——韩愈
It must be done out of one's own accord, without copying a single word from one's predecessors. — Han Yu

"必出于己，不袭蹈前人一言一句。"这句话出自唐代的诗人和思想家韩愈，意思是：自己的原创作品一定要来源于自己，不应该去抄袭之前其他人的创作，即使是一句话、一个词，都不要去有意地模仿。这句话强调的是写作的独立意识和创新精神，要求创作者能够根据自己的想法和方式独立地创作，不要重复别人已有的言论和内容，要做一个忠诚于自己的创作者。

"It must be done out of one's own accord, without copying a single word from one's predecessors." This quote is from Han Yu, a poet and thinker of the Tang Dynasty, and it means that one's original work must be out of oneself and should not copy what others have written before one, even if it is a sentence or a word, and should not be intentionally imitated. The phrase emphasises the sense of independence and creativity in writing, requiring the creator to be able to create independently according to his or her own ideas and ways, not to repeat what others have already said, and to be a creator who is true to himself or herself.

第三单元　校园生活篇
Unit 3 Campus Life

9 气象小主播的幕后工作 Weather anchor：behind the scenes

热身 WARMING UP

校园里一年一度的“百团大战”来啦，有汉服社、街舞社、滑板社……你想加入什么社团呢？

（图片来源：南信大社联公众号）

观看视频 WATCHING THE VIDEO

吴鹏飞同学加入了大学气象台，成为了一名“气象小主播”，为大家播报天气。让我们来看看他是怎么工作的吧！

扫描视频二维码观看

内容提示　CONTENT TIPS

Part 1

课文　text	生词　new words
气象小主播的幕后工作	幕后 mùhòu [adj.] behind the scenes, backstage
舍　友：你今天怎么没课？你准备去做什么？	
吴鹏飞：我今天九点要去拍摄“信大小主播”的节目。	拍摄 pāishè [v.] take (a picture), shoot 主播 zhǔbō [n.] anchor 节目 jiémù [n.] program
舍　友：今天可能会下雨，记得带把伞。	下雨 xiàyǔ [v.] rain, wetness
吴鹏飞：可是我的伞昨天坏掉了。	
舍　友：哎，没办法……今天我正好不出门，你用我的伞吧。	正好 zhènghǎo [adv.] just in time, exactly
吴鹏飞：OK，谢谢，我走了。	
（到拍摄地点后）	
吴鹏飞：稿件已经准备好了，可以开始拍摄了。	稿件 gǎojiàn [n.] manuscript
韦杰卓：大家好！我是信大气象小主播韦杰卓，今天由我为大家说天气……	准备 zhǔnbèi [v.] prepare, intend, ready

Part 2　注释　notes

1. 你今天怎么没课?

“怎么”用来询问原因、方式。例如：

“怎么” is used to ask for the reason or ways. For example:

① A：你怎么不回家？（询问原因）

B：我有事。

② A：你怎么不喝茶？（询问原因）
B：我不喜欢喝茶。
③ A：你怎么去学校？（询问方式）
B：我走路去学校。

2. 要

[能愿动词] 能愿动词是表示意愿、要求、可能、准许等的动词，如“要、可以、会、想”等。大多数能愿动词可以单独做谓语，可以用肯定、否定并列的形式表示疑问，可以受某些副词的修饰，不可以重叠。

[Modal verbs] Modal verbs are the verbs to express willing, requirements, possibilities or permissions，such as “要、可以、会、想” and so on. Most of modal verbs can be used as a predicate independently combination. They can be modified by some adverbs, but a modal verb cannot be geminated.

S	P①			
	Adv.		V	O
我		可以	帮	你
他	不	会	做	中国菜
大卫		要	去	超市
妹妹		想	学	画画

3. 可能

[副词] 表示估计。例如：

[adv.] “可能” expresses an estimation or assumption about someone or something. For example:

① 我可能五点吃晚饭。
② 明天可能不下雨。
③ 妈妈可能在家。

4. 会

[助动词] “会” 用在句中，表示可能，通常用于未发生的事件中。例如：

[Auxiliary verb] “会” is used in a sentence to indicate the possibility, usually referring to something that hasn't happened. For example:

---

① P 代表表语。

① 你不吃午饭会饿。
② 今天我会早点儿回家。
③ 明天我们可能会出去玩。

5. 拿把伞

表示“拿一把伞”，在口语表达中，数词“一”常常可以省略，其他数词不可以。例如：

It means "take an umbrella". In oral expression, the numeral "one" can often be omitted, and other numerals cannot. For example:

买一件衣服 = 买件衣服　　买两件衣服≠买件衣服
喝一杯水 = 喝杯水　　喝三杯水≠喝杯水
说一句话 = 说句话　　说几句话≠说句话

6. 可是我的伞坏掉了。

结果补语“掉”，无实义，用在动词、形容词的后面，表示动作的完成、状态的变化。例如：“他脱掉衣服了”表示动作的完成；“我的伞坏掉了”表示状态的变化。

The complement of result “掉”, which has no real meaning, follows verbs and adjectives to indicate the completion of actions and the change of state. For example, “他脱掉衣服了” indicates the completion of the action. “我的伞坏掉了” indicates the change of state.

综合练习　COMPREHENSIVE PRACTICE

Part 1　视频练习

看视频，选择填空　Watch the video and choose the best answer

1. 视频开头吴鹏飞在做什么？　（　　）

A. 读中文稿　　B. 读英文稿　　C. 读课文　　D. 读小说

2. 今天天气怎么样？ (　　)

A. 一直不下雨　　B. 已经下雨了　　C. 可能会下雨　　D. 可能不下雨

3. 吴鹏飞的伞怎么了？ (　　)

A. 忘在教室了　　B. 昨天坏掉了　　C. 借给朋友了　　D. 昨天不见了

4. 吴鹏飞的舍友今天要做什么？ (　　)

A. 不出门　　B. 要出门　　C. 不上课　　D. 要上课

看视频，回答问题　Watch the video and answer the questions

1. 吴鹏飞今天怎么没课？
2. 吴鹏飞最后出门带伞了吗？
3. “信大小主播”的工作是什么？

Part 2　书面练习

选词填空　Choose a word to fill in each blank

正好　　拍摄　　稿件　　主播　　准备

1. 你把餐具洗好，________吃饭，好吗？
2. 在饭店不远的地方，________有一家咖啡店，我们可以去喝咖啡。
3. 今天天气很好，很适合________视频。
4. 请你修改这一份________。
5. 新闻联播的________普通话很好。

完成句子　Complete the sentences

1. A：下午去看电影吗？
   B：对不起，____________________。（要）
2. 今天我很忙，____________________。（可能）
3. A：周末的天气怎么样？
   B：____________________。（会）
4. A：____________________？（怎么）
   B：我坐飞机回家。

连词成句　Match the words into a sentence

1. 生日　忘　我　了　妹妹　掉　的

____

2. 想　件　他　衣服　买

____

3. 宿舍　回　你　怎么

____

4. 聚会　周末　要　迈克　参加

____

Part 3　拓展练习

口语表达　Oral expression

1. 你看天气预报吗？什么时候会看天气预报？

2. 下周你和朋友打算去爬山，请你根据天气预报，和朋友商量一下你们要哪天出发。

复述课文 Repeat the text

吴鹏飞今天……，他……要去拍摄……的节目。他的舍友说今天……会……，让他记得……。可是吴鹏飞的伞……。舍友今天正好……，所以吴鹏飞用了……的伞。到了……后，吴鹏飞说稿件……，可以……。今天的……是韦杰卓，由她为大家……。

小组活动 Group work

3~4人一组，合作拍摄一个中文视频，拍摄内容自行选择，请做好分工记录。

提示词：视频拍摄、编写剧本、剪辑视频、参演人员

Video shooting, script writing, video editing, actors

记录表：

	名字	工作
1	马克	负责视频拍摄

文化链接 CULTURAL LINK

1. 气象 Weather, meteorology

发生在天空中的风、云、雨、雪等大气的物理现象。

Atmospheric physical phenomena such as wind, clouds, rain, and snow that occur in the sky.

（任泰 摄）

气象学 meteorology

大气现象 atmospheric phenomena

气象频道 the weather channel

气象主播 weather forecast announcer

（主播，指“主持人型播音员”the host type of announcer）

2. 二十四节气 The 24 Solar Terms

二十四节气，是我国历法中表示自然节律变化的特定节令。一年四季，春夏

秋冬各三个月，每个月有两个节气，每个节气均有其独特的含义。二十四节气准确地反映了自然节律变化，在人们日常生活中发挥了极为重要的作用。它不仅是指导农耕生产的时节体系，更是包含有丰富民俗事象的民俗系统。二十四节气蕴含着悠久的文化内涵和历史积淀，是中华民族悠久历史文化的重要组成部分。

（华培烨 摄）

The 24 solar terms are specific seasons in the calendar that express natural rhythm changes. Four seasons of the year, three months each in spring, summer, autumn and winter, two solar terms each month, each solar term has its own unique meaning. The 24 solar terms accurately reflect the changes in natural rhythms and play an extremely important role in people's daily lives. It is not only a season system for guiding agricultural production, but also a folklore system that contains rich folklore events.

The 24 solar terms contain a long cultural connotation and historical accumulation, and are an important part of the long history and culture of the Chinese nation.

（华培烨 摄）

按顺序排列分别是：

In order, they are:

① 立春 the Beginning of Spring
② 雨水 Rain Water
③ 惊蛰 the Waking of Insects
④ 春分 the Spring Equinox
⑤ 清明 Pure Brightness
⑥ 谷雨 Grain Rain
⑦ 立夏 the Beginning of Summer
⑧ 小满 Grain Full
⑨ 芒种 Grain in Ear
⑩ 夏至 the Summer Solstice
⑪ 小暑 Slight Heat
⑫ 大暑 Great Heat

⑬ 立秋 the Beginning of Autumn
⑭ 处暑 the Limit of Heat
⑮ 白露 White Dew
⑯ 秋分 the Autumnal Equinox
⑰ 寒露 Cold Dew
⑱ 霜降 Frost's Descent
⑲ 立冬 the Beginning of Winter
⑳ 小雪 Slight Snow
㉑ 大雪 Great Snow
㉒ 冬至 the Winter Solstice
㉓ 小寒 Slight Cold
㉔ 大寒 Great Cold

10 创业生活之加班
Entrepreneurial life of overtime

热身　WARMING UP

晚上八点，有人在操场上跑步，有人在图书馆学习，有人在宿舍看电视剧……你一般会做什么呢？和你的伙伴讨论一下吧。

跑步

学习

看剧

观看视频　WATCHING THE VIDEO

晚上八点，有一群学生还在办公室里，他们在干什么呢？我们一起去看看吧！

扫描视频二维码观看

内容提示 CONTENT TIPS

Part 1

课文 text	生词 new words
创业生活：加班	创业 chuàngyè [v.] start an undertaking
（同学 A 在和客户打电话）	加班 jiābān [v.] work overtime
	客户 kèhù [n.] customer
同学A：啊？丁总，你还在忙啊？	丁总 dīngzǒng [n.] Boss Ding
丁　总：对呀！我正在写一个策划案，准备推广我们的产品。	策划案 cèhuààn [n.] a plot 准备 zhǔnbèi [v.] prepare 推广 tuīguǎng [v.] popularize, spread 产品 chǎnpǐn [n.] product
同学A：那你吃饭了吗？	
丁　总：还没呢，等我忙完就去吃。	
同学A：好的，我也过来加班了。加油！	加油 jiāyóu [v.] make a greater effort
丁　总：我们一起加油啊！	
（星光不负赶路人）	

Part 2 注释 notes

1. 丁总

句中的“丁总”是一个昵称、外号。

“丁总”in the sentence is a nickname.

在中国，“姓氏 + 总”是一种职场称谓，一般表示总裁或总经理职位，现在也用来称呼外单位的客户或老板、本单位的领导等。

In China, "surname + general manager" is a workplace title, which generally indicates the position of president or general manager. Now it is also used to address customers or bosses of other units, leaders of this unit, etc.

2. 你还在忙啊？

[副词]“还”表示动作或者状态的持续。例如：

[adv.]“还”indicates the continuity of an action or a situation. For example:

① 他还在写作业。

② 明年我还在中国。

③ 她还每天跑步。

否定式用“还没”。例如：

Its negative form is“还没”. For example:

① 八点了，丁总还没吃饭。

② 我还没写完作业。

③ 我们还没开始上课。

3. 我正在写一个策划。

[副词] 动词的前面加上副词“正在”，表示动作的进行。例如：

[adv.] The processing of an action can be expressed by adding adverbs“正在”before a verb. For example:

① 我们正在上课。

② 妈妈正在看电视。

③ A：你在做什么？

B：我正在看书。

否定时可以直接用“没（有）”作简单回答。例如：

“没(有)”can be used as a negative reply. For example:

① A：你在吃饭吗？

B：没有，我正在写作业。

② A：你正在看电视吗？

B：我没在看电视。

4. 那你吃饭了吗？

[连词] 在口语中，“那”放在句首表示转移话题。例如：

[conj.] In Spoken Chinese,“那”at the beginning of a sentence indicates a change of subject. For example:

① A：我今天一直在上课。

B：那你想和我去看电影吗？

A：好啊。

② A：我想去北京旅游。

B：那你作业写完了吗？

A：还没呢。

5. 等我忙完就去吃。

“完”是结果补语，用在动词后，表示动作的结果。汉语中，一些动词（“完、懂、见”）或形容词（“好、干净”）可以放在动词后面，补充、说明动作的结果，它们叫结果补语。例如：

Used after a verb, a result complement indicates the result of an action. Some verbs(“完、懂、见”) or adjectives(“好、干净”) can be used after a verb to add remarks about the result of an action. They are called complements of result. For example:

S	V + Complement of result	O
我	写　完	作业了
她	听　懂	汉语课了
我	看　见	爸爸了
妈妈	做　好	晚饭了
大卫	洗　干净	衣服了

在结果补语前加“没（有）”表示否定，句尾不能用“了”。例如：

“没（有）” is added before the verb to form the negative form of a complement of result, in which case “了” cannot appear at the end of the sentence. For example:

S	没（有）+ V + Complement of result	O
我	没有　写　完	作业
她	没有　听　懂	汉语课
我	没　看　见	爸爸
妈妈	没　做　好	晚饭
大卫	没　洗　干净	衣服

[副词]“就”连接两个动词，表示两件事紧接着发生。前一个动作表示条件和原因，后一个动作表示结果。也可以用“一……就……”连接一个复句。例如：

[adv.] “就” connects two verbs, means two things happen one after another. The first action expresses the condition and cause, the second expresses the result. We can use “一……就……” connects a complex sentence. For example:

① 我吃完饭就睡觉了。

② 他写完作业就玩手机。

③ 我们一见面就说汉语。

6. 我也过来加班了。

[副词]“也”表示两事相同。例如：

[adv.] “也” means that two things are the same. For example:

① 马克学习汉语，我也学习汉语。

② 你在吃饭啊，我也在吃饭。

③ 你是学生，我也是。

综合练习　COMPREHENSIVE PRACTICE

Part 1　视频练习

将下列图片按顺序排列　Arrange the following pictures in order

A

B

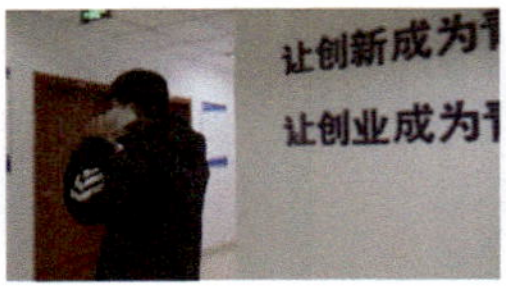

C

D

图片顺序为：________________________

看视频，选择填空　Watch the video and choose the best answer

1. 视频开头，同学 A 在和谁打电话？　(　　)

A. 丁总　　B. 李总　　C. 龙总

2. 视频里的“加班”是指什么时候？　(　　)

A. 早上　　B. 中午　　C. 晚上

3. 丁总在做什么？ （　　）

A. 做策划案　　B. 写作业　　C. 和客户聊天

4. 丁总吃饭了吗？ （　　）

A. 他正在吃饭　　B. 他还没吃饭　　C. 他吃完饭了

看视频，回答问题　Watch the video and answer the questions

1. 丁总为什么要写策划？
2. 看完了视频，你觉得加班的时候丁总和他的工作伙伴是什么样的心情？

Part 2　书面练习

选词填空　Choose a word to fill in each blank

创业　　加班　　策划　　准备　　加油

1. A：虽然这次的小组任务很难，但是我相信我们一定能完成。
   B：________！我们一起努力。
2. 已经十点了，他还在办公室________。
3. 杰克大学毕业了，但他不想找工作，他想自己________。
4. A：下周就是安妮的生日，你________好生日礼物了吗？
   B：当然啦。
5. 玛丽，这次的活动________就交给你来做了。

完成句子　Complete the sentences

1. A：我下午要去参加考试。

B：真巧啊，________________。（也）

2. A：他迟到了吗？

B：没有，现在________________。（还）

3. A：你________了吗？（完）

B：还没有。

4. A：我终于把所有的衣服洗完了。

B：________________________________？（那）

5. A：杰克在宿舍吗？他为什么不接我的电话？

B：________________________________，没听见。（正在）

连词成句　Match the words into a sentence

1. 下课　我　去　医院　一……就

____

2. 早餐　吃完　她　上学　去　就

____

3. 爸爸　回家　一……就　电视　看

____

4. 考完　就　我　试　吃饭　请你

____

5. 马丁　去　一……就　北京　到　故宫

____

Part 3　拓展练习

口语表达　Oral expression

同学们，你们加班过吗？请说一说你的加班经历。

提示词：……公司、……点上班、……点下班、为什么加班、加班多久

复述课文　Repeat the text

晚上……，同学A在和……打电话，丁总在写……案。

同学A打完电话走进办公室，他发现丁总还在……。丁总正在写……案，准备……他们的……。

同学A问丁总……了吗，丁总回答："……，等我……就……。"同学A说："好的，我也……了。……！"丁总说："我们……！"

小组活动 Group work

同学们，你们想过创业吗？假如你和你的伙伴现在准备创业，你们会去做什么呢？ 3~4 个人一组进行讨论，说一说你们的创业项目、创业计划。每组请一位同学报告情况。

记录表：

小组成员	创业项目	创业计划
珍妮	开奶茶店	先学习怎么制作奶茶，再选择开店地址，然后……

文化链接 CULTURAL LINK

1. 钉钉 DingTalk

钉钉是在中国企业中广泛使用的一个专业通信和协同办公平台，帮助企业和课堂降低沟通与管理成本，提升办公与教学效率。截至 2021 年 8 月 31 日，钉钉用户数已经突破 5 亿，包括企业、学校在内的各类组织数超过 1900 万。在新冠疫情期间，因为学校停课不停学的防疫政策，钉钉成为了中国老师与学生联系的主要平台。老师可以通过这一软件实时与学生互动并模拟现实课堂环境。钉钉等平台让无接触工作、学习成为可能，解决了疫情期间人员不能聚集的问题。

DingTalk is a professional communication and collaborative office platform widely used in Chinese enterprises, helping enterprises and classrooms to reduce communication and management costs and improve office and teaching efficiency. As of August 31, 2021, the number of DingTalk users has exceeded 500 million, and the number of organizations including enterprises and schools has exceeded 19 million. During the COVID-19 pandemic, DingTalk became the main platform for Chinese teachers to communicate with students due to the school's anti-epidemic policy of suspending classes. Teachers can use this software to interact with students in real time and simulate the real classroom environment. Platforms such as DingTalk make it possible to work and study without contact, and solve the problem that people cannot gather during the epidemic.

2. 腾讯会议 Tencent Meeting，TM

腾讯会议于 2019 年 12 月底上线，是提供实时共享屏幕、支持在线文档协作的一款音视频会议产品，同样在中国企业与各教育院校中广泛使用。与钉钉相同，这款软件也是疫情期间使用率很高的线上会议软件，为学生与办公人员提供了极大便利。但与钉钉不同的是，腾讯会议私密性更好，参会成员必须拥有会议号或会议邀请二维码才能参加一场腾讯会议，而钉钉会议中其他用户也可以自由加入。

Tencent Meeting was launched at the end of December 2019. It is an audio and video conference product that provides real-time screen sharing and supports online document collaboration. It is also widely used in Chinese enterprises and educational institutions. Like DingTalk, this software is also a highly used online conference software during the epidemic, which provides great convenience for students and office workers. But unlike DingTalk, Tencent Meeting are more private. Participants must have a conference ID or a conference invitation QR code to participate in a Tencent Meeting, and other users in the DingTalk conference can join freely.

3.“996”工作制 996 Work Schedule

“996”是一种高强度的工作制度。意思是工作日早上 9 点上班，晚上 9 点下班，中午休息 1 小时 (或不到 1 小时)，平均日工作时间总计 10 小时以上，每周工作 6 天。“996”工作制高于中国法定的工作强度，很多中国互联网公司年轻人的工作时间都是“996”。这个词语也常常被网友调侃为在工作中加班的代名词。

"996" is a high-intensity work system. It means working at 9:00 a.m. and leaving work at 9:00 p.m. on weekdays, 1 hour (or less than 1 hour) rest at noon, with an average daily working time of more than 10 hours in total, six days a week. The "996" work system is higher than the legal work intensity in China. Many Chinese youths in internet companies work in a 996 schedule. This term is often ridiculed by netizens as a synonym for working overtime at work.

11 走，一起去
Come on, let's go

热身 WARMING UP

同学们，你们喜欢旅游吗？当你们出去旅游的时候，你们会选择什么出行方式呢？是坐火车、高铁，还是坐飞机？

火车

高铁

飞机

观看视频 WATCHING THE VIDEO

校园里的四位同学想去食堂参加活动，他们会选择什么出行方式呢？让我们一起来看看吧！

扫描视频二维码观看

内容提示　CONTENT TIPS

Part 1

课文　text	生词　new words
走，一起去	
同学A：听说今天食堂有包饺子活动，你们想去参加吗？	包饺子 bāo jiǎo · zi [v.] make dumplings 参加 cānjiā [v.] join, attend, take part in
同学B：好呀。	
同学C：可以。	
同学D：你们都去吗？我不太想去……	
同学B：为什么呀？	
同学D：今天太热了，而且我宿舍离食堂很远，我不想走过去，还是算了吧。	热 rè [adj.] hot, heat 离 lí [v.] be apart [away] from, be at a distance from
同学C：现在校内交通很方便，要不你坐车去？	交通 jiāotōng [n.] traffic, transportation
同学A：对啊，如果你坐校园小公交的话，几分钟就到了。	公交 gōngjiāo [n.] bus
同学D：好主意！那我也去。你们打算怎么过去？	好主意 hǎo zhú · yi [n.] that's a good idea 打算 dǎsuàn [v.] to intend
同学B：食堂离我最近，我准备走过去。	
同学A：我想骑共享单车去，我买了优惠卡，相对来说很便宜。	共享单车 gòngxiǎng dānchē [n.] shared-bikes 优惠卡 yōuhuìkǎ [n.] courtesy card
同学C：我要滑滑板过去。	滑板 huábǎn [n.] skateboard
同学D：那走吧，我们一起出发！	出发 chūfā [v.] set out, start off

Part 2 注释 notes

1. ……还是算了吧。

“算了吧”常用于口语。“算了”做助词时用在句末，表达多一事不如少一事，并劝对方采纳某种做法，常表示祈使、劝说的语气。“算了”后面加语气词“吧”，使建议、劝说意味更强烈。

“算了吧” is often used in spoken language. When “算了吧” is used as an auxiliary word at the end of a sentence, it expresses that one thing is less desirable than another. And the speaker intends to persuade the other person not to take certain action by saying so. This phrase often indicates an imperative or persuasive tone. Adding the modal particle “吧” after “算了” intensifies the sense of suggestion or persuasion.

① A：明天要出去玩吗？
B：算了吧，我作业还没写完。

② A：我们要打车去电影院吗？
B：算了吧，电影院不远，我们走路去。

③ 今天一直下雨，出门还是算了吧。

2. 现在校内交通很方便，要不你坐车去？

“要不”是连词，后跟建议，用来委婉表达说话人的建议，以便获得听话人的同意。原因可以放在“要不”小句之前或之后。例如：

“要不”, followed by a suggestion, is a conjunction used to express the speaker's suggestion in a polite manner, so as to gain the agreement of the listener. The reason for the suggestion can be placed before or after the “要不” clause. For example:

① A：这周末去图书馆怎么样？
B：这周末我有事，要不下周末去吧。

② A：要不你先走吧，我还有点儿工作。
B：好的，明天见！

③ 我们要走快点儿，要不就迟到了。

3. 如果你坐校园小公交的话，几分钟就到了。

“如果……的话”这一分句表示假设，“就”后面的分句是在这种假设情况下产生的结果。注意，第二个分句的主语要放在“就”前面。例如：

The clause “如果……的话” indicates a hypothesis, and the clause following “就” is the result produced under this hypothetical situation. Note that the subject of the second clause should be placed before “就”. For example:

① 如果你很累的话，就休息一会儿。

② 如果你想学汉语的话，我就教你。

③ 如果有时间的话，我就去旅游。

4. 好主意！

“好主意”常用于口语，表示肯定、赞同别人提出的看法。例如：

“好主意” is often used in Spoken Chinese to express affirmation and approval of the opinion presented to others.For example：

① A：我们明天去吃广东菜怎么样？
B：好主意！我想吃广东菜很久了。

② A：我们吃完饭去散步吧？
B：好主意！还能顺便逛街。

③ A：你觉得我应该买衣服还是买裙子？
B：它们都很好看，你都买吧。
A：好主意！我都很喜欢。

5. 你们打算怎么过去？

“打算”表示考虑、计划做某事。例如：

“打算” means to consider or plan to do something. For example:

① A：你明天打算做什么？
B：我打算去运动。

② A：你打算什么时候吃饭？
B：我打算十二点去吃饭。

③ A：你打算走路回家吗？
B：我不打算走回去，我打算骑车。

6. 我买了优惠卡，相对来说很便宜。

“相对来说”用来表达说话者在和其他事物比较后对某个事物的看法。例如：

This pattern expresses the speaker's point of view after comparing with other options. For example:

① A：这件衣服居然卖一百块！
B：别的衣服更贵，这件相对来说还是便宜的。

② A：中国菜你觉得哪个比较好吃？
B：我觉得川菜相对来说好吃一点。

③ A：今天的作业好多啊！
B：昨天的作业更多，今天的相对来说已经很少了。

综合练习 COMPREHENSIVE PRACTICE

Part 1 视频练习

看视频，将句子和说话人的语气连线
Connect the following sentences with the speaker's tone

1. 你们想去参加吗？	A. 高兴 happy
2. 我不太想去……	B. 疑问 doubt
3. 还是算了吧。	C. 犹豫 hesitate
4. 要不你坐车去？	D. 劝说 persuade
5. 我们一起出发！	E. 建议 advise

看视频，选择填空 Watch the video and choose the best answer

1. 同学 D________去食堂，因为________。 (　　)
A. 不想走；今天虽然很凉快，但是宿舍离食堂太远了
B. 骑共享单车；今天很热，而且宿舍离食堂很远
C. 坐校园小公交；小公交很快，几分钟就到了

2. 同学 B 准备________去食堂，因为________。 (　　)
A. 走；食堂离他很近
B. 滑滑板；食堂离他很近
C. 走；今天很凉快

3. 同学 C 要________去食堂。 (　　)
A. 骑自行车　　B. 滑滑板　　C. 滑轮滑

4. 同学 A 打算________去食堂，因为________。 (　　)
A. 骑自行车；他买了优惠卡，相对来说很便宜
B. 骑共享单车；他买了优惠卡，相对来说不贵
C. 骑共享单车；他买了优惠卡，相对来说很便宜

看视频，回答问题 Watch the video and answer the questions

1. 视频中，同学 D 的态度经历了几次变化？为什么？
2. 视频的最后，同学们一起出发去做什么？

3. 看完视频，总结一下校园里有哪些交通工具，并补充你知道的其他交通工具。

Part 2　书面练习

选词填空　Choose a word to fill in each blank

听说　　参加　　打算　　优惠　　离　　好主意

1. A：这周末你要去做什么？
   B：我________去图书馆学习。
2. ________学校礼堂周三有音乐会，我们一起去吧！
3. 我准备八月份________HSK 四级的考试。
4. A：我最近想买衣服了，我们一起去逛街吧。
   B：周五商场有很多________活动，衣服会很便宜，我们周五去怎么样？
   A：哦，这真是一个________。
5. 我家________学校很远，骑车大概 1 个小时。

完成句子　Complete the sentences

1. A：新年要到了，你________________________？（询问计划）
   B：我________________________________。（回答计划）
2. A：今天 35 ℃，西安的夏天太热了吧！
   B：杭州今天 42 ℃ 呢，西安的夏天________________。（相对来说）
3. A：我们怎么去北京呀？
   B：飞机票好贵啊，____________________________？（要不……）
4. A：安塞腰鼓课全校就 30 个名额，好难抢啊！
   B：____。（算了吧）
5. A：我的头好痛啊……
   B：__________________________________。（如果……的话，就……）

句子配对　Match the sentences

1. 周五商场打折，你打算买什么？
2. 要是你有时间的话，
3. 杰克怎么还不来，电影快开始了。
4. 情人节我们去卖花吧！
5. 太晚了，地铁都没有了。

A. 好主意，一定能赚很多钱。
B. 要不我们打车回去？
C. 我打算买台电脑和一些衣服。
D. 算了吧，我们别等他了。
E. 就来我们学校，我请你吃饭。

Part 3 拓展练习

双人活动 Pair work

两人一组，根据表格互相提问并回答。

	问题	回答
1	如果有时间的话，你打算做什么？	如果有时间的话，我就去旅游。
2	如果有很多钱的话，你打算做什么？	如果……的话，我就……
3	如果朋友生日到了的话，你打算送什么？	
4	如果明天下雨的话，你打算做什么？	
5	如果你是超人的话，你打算做什么？	

复述课文 Repeat the text

同学 A：听说今天……有……活动，你们想去……吗？
同学 B：……。
同学 C：……。
同学 D：你们……？我……想去……
同学 B：……呀？
同学 D：今天……，而且我宿舍……，我不想……，还是……。
同学 C：现在校内……很……，要不……？
同学 A：对啊，如果……的话，……就……。
同学 D：……！那我也去。你们……怎么过去？
同学 B：食堂……，我准备……。
同学 A：我想……去，我买了……，相对来说……。
同学 C：我要……过去。
同学 D：那走吧，我们……！

口语表达 Oral expression

如果你的中国朋友想去你的国家旅游，请你给出一些旅游建议，如应什么时候去、哪些景点值得去、出行方式有哪些。

提示：交通工具（火车、汽车、飞机、轮船……）

文化链接 CULTURAL LINK

1. 高铁 High Speed Rail

高铁是高速铁路的简称，是指设计标准等级高、可供列车安全高速行驶的铁路系统。世界上第一条正式的高速铁路系统是日本东海道新干线，1964 年建成，通车的时速为 200 km/h。而随着科技发展，目前中国高铁时速均超过 250 km/h。截至 2020 年底，中国铁路营业里程达 14.6 万 km，高速铁路运营里程达 3.79 万 km，稳居世界第一。高速铁路极大方便了中国人出行。有了高铁，春运压力极大缓解。大学生的寒暑假回家之路也更加顺畅。中国高铁不断借鉴国内外的铁路经验，并坚持自主研发创新，最终运营达到了世界顶尖水平。

High-speed rail is the abbreviation for high-speed railway, which refers to a railway system with a high design standard level for trains to travel safely and at high speed. The first official high-speed railway system in the world was the Tokaido Shinkansen in Japan, which was completed in 1964 and opened to traffic at a speed of 200 km/h. And with the development of technology, China's high-speed railways now all have a speed of over 250 km/h. By the end of 2020, China's railway mileage was 146000 km, with 37900 km of high-speed railways in operation, ranking firmly as the first in the world. High-speed railways have greatly facilitated the travel of Chinese people. With the high-speed railway, the pressure of the Spring Festival has been greatly relieved. The journey home for university students during the winter and summer holidays has also become smoother. China's high-speed railways continue to learn from the railway experience at home and abroad, and insist on independent research and innovation, and eventually the operation has reached the world's top level.

2. 共享单车 Shared-Bikes

共享单车指的是自行车出行共享经济服务。在中国很多城市，无论是校园、地铁站点、公交站点，还是居民区、商业区、公共服务区，人们都可以看到外形相似、色彩独特的自行车。用户只要扫描车身的二维码，并根据手机提示操作，就可以解锁并骑行。而到达指定停车地点归还自行车后，用户就能完成一次低碳出行。共享单车可以解决短程路途的用车问题，也为环保事业做出了不小的贡献。共享单车软件在 2016 年底呈现爆发增长态势，但也出现了许多问题。随着近年来行业逐步规范，许多共享单车品牌找到了健康的现金管理方式，以租金为主要收入来源，实现了盈利。

Shared-bikes refer to the economic service of sharing bicycle travel. In many cities in China, people can see bicycles with similar shapes and unique colours, whether on campuses, underground stations, bus stops, or in residential, commercial or public service areas. Users can unlock and ride the bikes by scanning the QR code on the body and following the mobile phone prompts. And after arriving at the designated parking spot to return the bike, users can complete a low–carbon trip. Bicycle sharing can solve the problem of using bicycles for short road journeys, and also makes a considerable contribution to environmental protection. Shared–bikes software showed explosive growth at the end of 2016, but many problems have also emerged. As the industry has been gradually regulated in recent years, many shared–bikes brands have found a healthy way to manage their cash and become profitable with rentals as their main source of income.

12 网购真方便
Online shopping is so convenient

热身　WARMING UP

在西方，每年的“黑色星期五”商家都会给出非常优惠的促销价格；在中国，每年的“双十一”也有巨大的优惠，人们会趁这个机会疯狂地购物。那么在你的国家，有没有购物节呢？

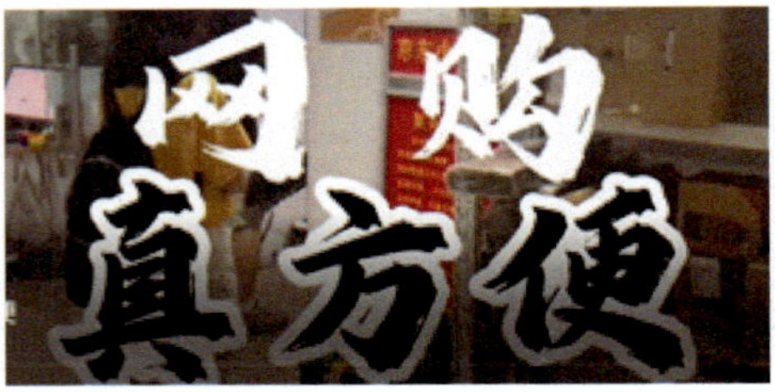

观看视频　WATCHING THE VIDEO

“双十一”购物节快到了，同学 A 和同学 B 准备网购，他们打算买什么呢？我们一起来看看吧！

扫描视频二维码观看

内容提示 CONTENT TIPS

Part 1

课文 text	生词 new words
网购真方便	网购 wǎnggòu [n.] online shopping
（同学 A 和同学 B 在宿舍）	
同学A：你在干什么？	
同学B：“双十一”购物节快到了，淘宝上有很多优惠活动，我在找要买的东西。	购物节 gòu wù jié [n.] Shopping Festival 淘宝 táobǎo [n.] an online shopping APP in China 优惠 yōuhuì [adj.] preferential, favourable
同学A：你提醒我了，我正好也想买几件新衣服。	提醒 tíxǐng [v.] call attention to, remind 正好 zhènghǎo [adv.] just, exactly
……	
同学A：你帮我选一选，这件衣服哪个颜色适合我？	适合 shìhé [v.] suit
同学B：我觉得黑色的很日常，白色的更百搭一点儿。	日常 rìcháng [adj.] daily 百搭 bǎidā [adj.] easy matching
同学A：那我买这件白色的吧！	
（两天后）	
同学B：呀！我前天买的东西今天就到了，你的呢？	
同学A：我的也是，好快啊！	
同学B：我们一起去拿快递吧！	快递 kuàidì [n.] express delivery
（同学 A 和同学 B 在快递站）	
同学A：好多人啊，平时都没有这么多人。	平时 píngshí [n.] in normal times 趁 chèn [perp.] while

同学B：是啊，因为大家都喜欢趁有优惠的时候买东西，而且现在网购那么方便，所以这两天的快递特别多。

同学A：对哦～那我们赶快去排队吧！

赶快 gǎnkuài [adv.] at once, quickly

排队 páiduì [v.] form a line, line up

Part 2　注释　notes

1. "双十一"购物节快到了。

"快……了"表示动作或事件即将发生。例如：

"快……了" indicates that an action or event is about to happen. For example:

① 快到圣诞节了，你们有什么活动吗？

② 我们快到学校了。

③ 我们班快考试了。

2. 正好

[副词]"正好"表示恰好或遇到某个机会做某事。例如：

[adv.]"正好" means "it is the right time or opportunity to do something". For example:

① 我看书的时候他正好来了。

② 妈妈叫我吃饭的时候，我正好写完作业。

③ 朋友送的生日礼物正好是我想要的东西。

3. 适合

[动词]"适合"意思是"相配、符合"，在汉语中往往说"什么东西适合另一种东西"，后面一般要接宾语。例如：

[v.]"适合" means "to match", and in Chinese, it is often said that "something is suitable for another thing", which is generally followed by an object. For example:

① 这条裙子适合玛丽，不适合你。

② 他适合当汉语老师。

③ 今天天气很好，适合出门。

4. 我觉得黑色的很日常。

"黑色的"是"的"字短语，在句中表示"黑色的衣服"。名词、代词、动词、形容词等后面加"的"可以构成"的"字短语，相当于省略了中心语的名称短语。例如：

“黑色的”is a“的”phrase, which in a sentence indicates“黑色的衣服”(i.e. "black clothes"). Nouns, pronouns, verbs, adjectives, and others followed by“的”can form a“的”phrase, which is equivalent to an elliptical nominal phrase where the head-word is omitted. For example:

① 这本书不是我的。= 这本书不是我的书。

② 这件衣服是昨天买的。= 这件衣服是昨天买的衣服。

③ 这两个杯子，绿色的是我的。= 绿色的杯子是我的杯子。

N + 的	P + 的	V + 的	Adj. + 的
中国的	我的	吃的	长的
朋友的	你的	喝的	短的
上海的	他的	跑步的	新的
爸爸的	我们的	走路的	蓝色的

5. 白色的更百搭一点儿。

“更……一点儿”用在表示比较的句子中。“更”是程度副词，表示一种比较，“一点儿”表示比较的程度稍有差别。例如：

“更……一点儿”is used in sentences that express comparison.“更”is a adverb of degree that indicates a comparison, while“一点儿”suggests that the degree of comparison is slightly different. For example:

① A：你觉得咖啡和茶哪个好喝？
B：我觉得咖啡更好喝一点儿。

② A：你喜欢英国还是美国？
B：我更喜欢英国一点儿。

③ A：这两个女生谁更漂亮？
B：我觉得左边的更漂亮一点儿。

6. 我前天买的东西今天就到了。

[副词]“就”是时间副词，强调说话人认为事情发生得早，进行得快、顺利。例如：

[adv] It is used for emphasis, indicating that the speaker thinks something happened early or went fast and well. For example:

① 八点上课，艾伦七点就到教室了。

② 从南京坐飞机到北京就两个小时。

③ 我十分钟就写完作业了。

7. 因为大家都喜欢趁有优惠的时候买东西。

[介词] "趁" 表示利用某种条件或某个机会做某事，常用在口语中。"趁" 字后面可以跟名词、动词短语、形容词和小句。例如：

The word "趁" indicates taking advantage of certain conditions or an opportunity to do something. It is commonly used in spoken language. After the character " 趁 " , one can use nouns, verb phrases, adjectives, and clauses. For example:

① 早餐要趁热吃。

② 趁今天不下雨，我们去公园吧。

③ 趁电影还没开始，我去买些吃的。

8. 赶快

[副词] "赶快" 表示抓紧时间、加快速度。例如：

[adv.] "赶快" means to seize the time and speed up. For example:

① 火车马上就要出发了，我们要赶快上车。

② 下节课就要交作业了，你赶快写作业。

③ 快考试了，赶快复习吧。

综合练习 COMPREHENSIVE PRACTICE

Part 1 视频练习

看视频，判断对错 Watch the video and judge true or false

1. 同学 A 根本不知道 "双十一" 购物节。 ( )
2. 同学 B 想在 "双十一" 的时候买几件衣服。 ( )
3. 同学 A 最后买了白色的衣服。 ( )
4. 同学 B 是昨天买的东西。 ( )
5. 同学 A 的快递今天还没到。 ( )
6. 看见快递站那么多人，同学 A 觉得很平常。 ( )

看视频，选择填空 Watch the video and choose the best answer

1. 视频开头，同学 B 在做什么？ ( )

A. 在手机上看视频

B. 刷淘宝，找要买的东西

C. 在手机上和朋友聊天

2. “双十一”购物节的时候买东西，和平时相比________。 (   )

A. 更贵了

B. 更便宜

C. 价格不变

3. 关于衣服，同学 B 觉得________很日常，________更百搭一点儿。(   )

A. 黑色的；白色的

B. 白色的；黑色的

C. 黑色的；灰色的

4. 看见快递站那么多人，同学 A 和同学 B________。 (   )

A. 马上就走了

B. 让同学帮忙拿快递

C. 赶快去排队了

看视频，回答问题 Watch the video and answer the questions

1. 视频中，“双十一”是什么日子？和平时有什么不一样吗？
2. 为什么快递站有那么多人？

Part 2 书面练习

选词填空 Choose a word to fill in each blank

赶快 网购 平时 日常 适合 正好

1. A：我打算去超市买东西。

   B：________我也要去，我们一起走吧。
2. 情人节快到了，我想选一件________男朋友的礼物。
3. A：我们家怎么每天都有这么多快递？

   B：因为妈妈最近爱上了________，每天买好多东西。
4. 过节的时候，景区的人很多，________人不多。
5. A：快来帮我选一选，哪个颜色更好看？

   B：绿色的不太________，我觉得白色的更好。
6. 我们________走，上课就要迟到了。

完成句子 Complete the sentences

1. A：________________________________。(赶快)

B：好，我马上就写完了。

2. A：我好想去看明天的球赛啊，可是票已经卖完了。
   B：________________，我们可以一起去。（正好）
3. A：这是你的自行车吗？
   B：不，________________。（“的”字短语）
   A：那你的是什么颜色的？
   B：________________。（“的”字短语）
4. ________________，我们一起去听音乐会吧。（趁）
5. 这两套餐具，我觉得________________。（更……一点儿）

句子配对　Match the sentences

1. 快到端午节了，
2. 时间不早了，
3. 趁肯德基有优惠活动，
4. 正好今天是妈妈的生日，
5. 小马跑得比小王更快一点儿，

A. 我们去买些吃的吧。
B. 这次比赛更适合小马参加。
C. 我们赶快回家吧。
D. 我为她买了一个大蛋糕。
E. 我们可以去划龙舟。

Part 3　拓展练习

口语表达　Oral expression

用“的”字短语回答问题。

例如：我的鞋子是黑色的。

1. 你的上衣是什么颜色？
2. 你的裤子是什么颜色？
3. 坐在你前面的是谁？
4. 坐在你后面的是谁？
5. 班里会打篮球的是谁？

复述课文　Repeat the text

（同学 A 和同学 B 在宿舍）

同学 A：你在……？

同学 B：……快到了，……上有很多……，我在找……。

同学 A：你……我了，我……也想买……。

……

同学 A：你帮我……，这件衣服……我？

同学 B：我觉得……很……，……更……一点儿。

同学 A：那我买……吧！

（两天后）

同学 B：呀！我……买的东西……，你的呢？

同学 A：我的……，好快啊！

同学 B：我们一起……吧！

（同学 A 和同学 B 在快递站）

同学 A：好多人啊，……都没有……。

同学 B：是啊，因为大家……趁……买东西，而且现在……那么……，所以这两天的……。

同学 A：对哦～那我们……去……吧！

小组活动　Group work

3~4 人一组，互相询问并记录小组成员的网购情况，每组请一位同学报告情况。

记录表：

	名字	是否网购过	网购平台	购买的东西
1	珍妮	是	淘宝	衣服、化妆品

文化链接　CULTURAL LINK

1. 淘宝　Taobao

"淘宝"一般指的是淘宝网，是中国目前最受欢迎的网络购物平台之一。作为亚洲范围内最大的购物网站，淘宝开创了一种非常方便、高效的购物模式。在淘宝不断优化和发展的过程中，越来越多的卖家能够通过这个平台吸引消费者，获得新的发展机会；而消费者们也可以有更多、更优的产品选择空间。用户可以通过关键词检索或者拍照搜索等多种方式，在淘宝上寻找自己想要的产品，填写地址、付款，就可以在家中等待收取产品包裹，如果对产品不满意，也能很方便地把产品退回。

Taobao generally refers to Taobao.com, one of the most popular online shopping platforms in China today. As the largest shopping site within Asia, Taobao has created a very convenient and efficient shopping model. As Taobao continues to optimise and develop, more and more sellers are able to use the platform to attract consumers and gain new opportunities for growth, while consumers have more and better choices of products to choose from. Users can search for the products they want on Taobao in a variety of ways, such as through keyword searches or photo searches, fill in their addresses, make payments, and wait to receive their product parcels at home, or easily return the products if they are not satisfied with them.

2.“双十一”：从光棍节到购物节
Double Eleven: From a bachelor's day to a shopping festival

“双十一”指的是淘宝在每年11月11日举行的网上购物活动。11月11日本来是中国年轻人的光棍节，因为这一天日期里有四个阿拉伯数字“1”，就像四根光滑的棍子。“光棍”在汉语里的意思是“单身”。为了吸引更多的年轻消费者，淘宝网从2009年起，每年光棍节这一天，都会举行“双十一”促销活动，以鼓励网友购物。随着淘宝网的不断推广、宣传，“双十一”这个日子已经由光棍节成功转变为全民购物节。最近几年，“双十一”成交额均在2000亿元以上，远超“黑色星期五”和“网络星期一”。今天的“双十一”更像是一场狂欢，人们在这一天观看购物晚会、带货直播，在购物的同时，体验线上的娱乐氛围。

"Double Eleven" refers to the online shopping event held by Taobao on November 11, which is traditionally known as One's Day for young Chinese people because of the four Arabic numbers "1" in the date, which resembles four smooth sticks. The Chinese word for "bachelor" means "single". In order to attract more young consumers, Taobao.com has held a "Double 11" promotion every year since 2009 to encourage online shoppers to shop on the day of Hanukkah. With Taobao's continuous promotion and publicity, Double Eleven has been successfully transformed from a bachelor's day to a national shopping festival. In recent years, the turnover of Double Eleven has been above 200 billion, far exceeding that of Black Friday and Cyber Monday. Today's Double Eleven is more of a carnival, with people watching shopping parties and live streaming of goods, and experiencing online entertainment while shopping.

（答案仅供参考）

答　案　册
Reference answers

1 校园里的相遇
Encounters on campus

综合练习 COMPREHENSIVE PRACTICE

Part 1 视频练习

看视频，判断对错 Watch the video and judge true or false

1. √　2. ×　3. ×　4. ×　5. √

看视频，选择填空 Watch the video and choose the best answer

1.A　2.C　3.B　4.B

看视频，回答问题 Watch the video and answer the questions

1. 为什么她们的生活平平无奇？

引导学生根据“平平无奇”的意思进行回答，如因为她们的生活没什么特别的活动，总是一个人起床、运动、吃饭。

2. 米雅和韦杰卓认识后去做了什么？

她们认识后一起去上课、放风筝、拍照、吃中国美食、剪纸。

3. 米雅为什么越来越喜欢中国了？

因为韦杰卓教她中文，带她做了很多有趣的事情，让她更加了解中国。

Part 2 书面练习

选词填空 Choose a word to fill in each blank

1. 相遇　2. 平平无奇　3. 给　4. 了解　5. 美食

完成句子 Complete the sentences

引导学生根据实际情况回答，答案仅供参考。

1. 我是汉语国际教育专业的学生。
2. 我来中国差不多 2 年了。
3. 我越来越喜欢运动。
4. 我们班来了一位新同学，我给你介绍一下。

连词成句 Match the words into a sentence

1. 小王给我一瓶水。/ 我给小王一瓶水。
2. 他教安娜画画。/ 安娜教他画画。
3. 妈妈告诉我一个好消息。/ 我告诉妈妈一个好消息。
4. 大家叫他李老师。

Part 3 拓展练习

复述课文 Repeat the text

韦杰卓是汉语国际教育专业的学生，她来南信大两年了。米雅来南信大学习国际贸易，差不多三年了。她们的生活平平无奇，直到有一天她们在课堂上相遇了。她们相遇后，会一起去拍照、放风筝、吃美食、剪纸。韦杰卓喜欢给米雅拍好看的照片，教她中文，介绍中国文化。认识韦杰卓以后，米雅吃到了很多中国美食，了解了很多中国文化，她越来越喜欢中国了。

2 开始上课了 Class begins

综合练习 COMPREHENSIVE PRACTICE

Part 1 视频练习

看视频，判断对错 Watch the video and judge true or false

1.× 2.× 3.× 4.× 5.√

看视频，选择填空 Watch the video and choose the best answer

1.B 2.C 3.A 4.C 5.B

看视频，回答问题 Watch the video and answer the questions

1. 同学A认为美是什么？为什么？

同学A认为美就是我们自己，柏拉图说“美是难的”，因为认识你自己本身就是难的。

2. 大家认为同学A的观点是对的吗？为什么？

大家同意她的观点，因为视频结尾的时候同学们给予了同学A热烈的掌声。

Part 2 书面练习

选词填空 Choose a word to fill in each blank

1. 报名 2. 善良 3. 有意思 4. 材料；讨论 5. 认为

完成句子 Complete the sentences

引导学生根据实际情况回答，答案仅供参考。

1. 我每天又要学习又要工作。
2. 我觉得又便宜又好吃。
3. 夏天挺热的，不用穿很多衣服。
4. 这部电影我很喜欢，我觉得挺好看的。
5. 寒假的时候，我去北京了。

从字到词 From Chinese characters to words

1. 略
2. 美丽 我的家乡很美丽。
   美味 妈妈做的饭很美味。
   精美 中国瓷器非常精美。

Part 3 拓展练习

复述课文 Repeat the text

上课前，刘老师在班级群里发了一份阅读材料，叫作《大希庇阿斯篇》，还说下节课要请几位同学讨论这篇文章。同学A觉得还挺有意思的，问大家要去报名吗。

上课的时候，刘老师问同学们美是什么，同学们开始了讨论。

同学B说美是善良，善良就是好人。同学C觉得美是妈妈的脸，同学D认为美是好看。

最后，同学A认为美就是我们自己，柏拉图说“美是难的”，因为认识你自己就是难的。大家认为她说的是对的。

3 今天吃什么？ What to eat today？

综合练习 COMPREHENSIVE PRACTICE

Part 1 视频练习

看视频，判断对错 Watch the video and judge true or false

1.× 2.× 3.√ 4.× 5.×

看视频，选择填空 Watch the video and choose the best answer

1.B 2.B 3.C 4.A

看视频，回答问题 Watch the video and answer the questions

1. 同学A推荐了哪些中国菜？

同学A推荐了川菜。

2. 同学B去吃川菜了吗？为什么？

同学B没有去吃川菜，因为不能吃辣。

3. 为什么同学A晚上吃得很少？

因为同学A晚上习惯吃少点。中国人常说“早上吃得好，中午吃得饱，晚上吃得少”。

Part 2 书面练习

选词填空 Choose a word to fill in each blank

1. 推荐；价格 2. 顺便 3. 习惯 4. 种类；口味 5. 便宜

完成句子　Complete the sentences

1. 他不仅会说，而且说得很好。
2. 原来是这样啊。
3. 你可以查查地图或问一问路人。
4. 今天的天气是不是不太好？
5. 假期快到了，你是不是准备去旅游？

连词成句　Match the words into a sentence

1. 玛丽不但喜欢唱歌（跳舞），而且喜欢跳舞（唱歌）。
2. 杰克不但是作家，还是运动员。
3. 云南不但风景很美，食物也很好吃。
4. 不但安娜会唱歌，而且玛丽也会唱歌。
5. 不但我会做中国菜，我的朋友也会做。

Part 3　拓展练习

复述课文　Repeat the text

（早上）

同学A：早餐你想吃什么？

同学B：我想要一个肉包和一个茶叶蛋，你呢？

同学A：我想要一杯豆浆和一根油条。

（中午）

同学B：我昨天中午吃了西餐，今天想吃中国菜，你有什么推荐的吗？

同学A：我觉得川菜很好吃，你可以去试试。

同学B：川菜是不是很辣？我不能吃辣，还有别的吗？

同学A：是的，川菜比较辣。你还可以去快餐窗口看看，那里的菜不但种类多，而且价格便宜。

同学B：好的，我去看看。

同学A：明天我想尝尝西餐，你有什么建议吗？

同学B：我喜欢吃黑椒口味的意面，还有牛排。你可以试试。

（晚上）

同学B：你晚上怎么吃得这么少？最近在减肥吗？

同学A：不是的，我晚上习惯吃少点。因为中国人常说"早上吃得好，中午吃得饱，晚上吃得少"。

同学B：原来是这样啊。以后我晚上也要少吃点，还能顺便减肥呢！

4 你在哪儿？ Where are you？

综合练习 COMPREHENSIVE PRACTICE

Part 1 视频练习

看视频，判断对错 Watch the video and judge true or false

1.× 2.× 3.√ 4.× 5.×

看视频，选择填空 Watching video and choose the best answer

1. C 2. B 3. A 4.C

看视频，回答问题 Watch the video and answer the questions

1. 同学 B 的家乡在哪儿？同学 A 知道了后，有什么反应？

同学 B 的家乡在苏州，同学 A 听说苏州园林很有名，想去见识见识。

2. 视频的最后，同学 A 和同学 B 约定了什么？

他们约定，有机会的话一起去苏州玩儿。

Part 2 书面练习

选词填空 Choose a word to fill in each blank

1. 机会；一言为定 2. 宿舍 3. 家乡 4. 有名；见识 5. 建筑

完成句子 Complete sentences

1. 有机会的话，我们一起去海边玩吧！

2. 我们学校会提供宿舍，那你的学校呢？
3. 我很累，想回去休息一下。
4. 听说最近有新电影上映，你想去看看吗？
5. 你现在在哪儿？
   我在练习跑步。

连词成句　Match the words into a sentence

1. 我们下周一起去公园野餐吧！
2. 我明天要去图书馆学习。
3. 安娜骑自行车上学。
4. 杰克用电脑写作业。
5. 我放学后要回家休息。

Part 3　拓展练习

复述课文　Repeat the text

（同学 A 和同学 B 在打电话）

同学A：喂，XXX，我们一起去教室上课吧？

同学B：好呀。

同学A：你现在在哪儿？ 我去找你吧。

同学B：我在宿舍。

同学A：你的宿舍在哪儿？

同学B：在晖园12栋。

同学A：知道了，你在宿舍等一下。

（同学 A 和同学 B 见面了）

同学B：我们今天在哪儿上课？

同学A：在文德楼301，今天上的是文化课“中国民居”。

同学B：中国民居？ 那你的家乡在哪儿？

同学A：我家在北京。

同学B：哦~我知道北京有四合院。

同学A：那你家呢？

同学B：我家在苏州，你了解苏州的建筑吗？

同学A：听说苏州园林很有名，真想去见识见识。

同学B：有机会的话，我们一起去苏州玩儿！

同学A：好呀，一言为定！

5 有意思的体育课 Interesting PE classes

综合练习 COMPREHENSIVE PRACTICE

Part 1 视频练习

看视频，将句子和说话人的语气连线 Connect the following sentences with the speaker's tone

1.E 2.C 3.D 4.A 5.B

看视频，选择填空 Watch the video and choose the best answer

1.C 2.B 3.A 4.C

看视频，回答问题 Watch the video and answer the questions

1. 视频中，同学 A 对太极课的看法有哪些变化？

同学 A 一开始觉得太极听起来好有意思；看了视频后，认为太极看起来好轻松；听了同学 B 的解释，明白了太极的一招一式都有讲究，要练好可不容易。

2. 结合视频，介绍一下安塞腰鼓这门体育课。

根据视频，安塞腰鼓是中国陕北的传统体育活动，而且全校就 30 个名额，非常难抢。

3. 视频里出现了哪些体育活动，你觉得哪种运动最有意思？

（师生一起总结视频中出现的体育运动，并引导学生流利地说出自己的看法。）

Part 2 书面练习

选词填空 Choose a word to fill in each blank

1. 选课　2. 名额　3. 体育；有意思　4. 轻松　5. 讲究　6. 传统

完成句子 Complete the sentences

1. 他说得可好了。
2. 才不是呢，我不会这么早结婚的。
3. 看起来还不错。
4. 这几天挺冷的，你应该多穿一点。
5. 我不是不想参加同学聚会，的确是没有时间。

句子配对 Match the sentences

1.B　2.D　3.E　4.F　5.A　6.C

Part 3 拓展练习

复述课文 Repeat the text

同学A：这学期的体育课你选课了吗？

同学B：我抢到了太极课。

同学A：太极，听起来好有意思。

同学B：我也觉得，给你看看我们的上课视频。

同学A：哇，看起来好轻松。

同学B：才不是呢，太极的一招一式都有讲究，要练好可不容易。

同学A：原来如此。

同学B：那你选了什么课？

同学A：我选了安塞腰鼓课，全校就30个名额，别提多难抢了！

同学B：安塞腰鼓？这是什么？

同学A：安塞腰鼓是中国陕北的传统体育活动，我觉得还挺有意思的。

同学B：打鼓应该挺累的吧？

同学A：的确很累，但也很好玩儿！我觉得体育课是最有意思的课了。

同学B：我也喜欢上体育课。

6 气象小主播之芒种 Weather anchor: Grain in Ear

综合练习 COMPREHENSIVE PRACTICE

Part 1 视频练习

看视频，判断对错 Watch the video and judge true or false

1.× 2.√ 3.√ 4.× 5.√

看视频，选择填空 Watching video and choose the best answer

1.C 2.B 3.B 4.A

看视频，回答问题 Watch the video and answer the questions

1. 本期天气预报主要介绍了什么？

（让学生用自己的话总结全文，回答合理即可）本期天气预报介绍了芒种期间的天气、芒种的独特含义以及高考期间的气候情况。

2. 为什么高考会安排在芒种期间？

因为这段时间是我国夏季气候条件最好的时候，也有利于高考的组织和考试工作，以及各大高校的招生、录取工作。

3. 为什么说“芒种与高考密不可分”？

（引导学生理解“密不可分”的意思和芒种蕴含的独特意义）因为芒种包含“一收一种”的含义，就像高考，有付出才有回报，有播种方有收获。

Part 2 书面练习

选词填空 Choose a word to fill in each blank

1. 巧合 2. 持续 3. 密不可分 4. 一年一度 5. 组织 6. 独特

完成句子 Complete sentences

1. 我认为学习汉语要多听、多读以及多说。
2. 明天的生日会由杰克安排。
3. 我觉得送礼物并非越贵越好。

4. 暑假我将去北京旅游。

连词成句 Match the words into a sentence

1. 前面就是图书馆。
2. 我就坐在教室。
3. 努力就有收获。
4. 我就不写作业。

Part 3 拓展练习

复述课文 Repeat the text

大家好！我是气象小主播张文杉，今天由我为大家说天气。

水国芒种后，梅天风雨凉。时间飞快，小满之后紧接着是芒种，以及一年一度的高考。芒种以及之后几天，将会一直持续多云，温度为 27~32℃，体感温度较热。同学们应做好防晒，避免中暑。

高考安排在芒种期间并非巧合，因为这段时间是我国夏季气候条件最好的时候，也有利于高考的组织和考试工作，以及各大高校的招生、录取工作。

作为最独特的二十四节气，芒种与高考密不可分，包含“一收一种”的含义，就像高考，有付出才有回报，有播种方有收获。

本期天气预报就到这里，我们下期再见。

7 我的室友是网络作家 My roommate is an internet writer

综合练习 COMPREHENSIVE PRACTICE

Part 1 视频练习

看视频，将句子和说话人的语气连线 Connect the following sentences with the speaker's tone

1.B 2.C 3.D 4.A

看视频，选择填空 Watch the video and choose the best answer

1.C　2.C　3.B　4.A

看视频，回答问题 Watch the video and answer the questions

1. 你知道谁是小说的作者吗？同学 A 知道吗？

（学生理解整个视频内容后再作答）同学 B 是小说的作者，同学 A 不知道。

2. 同学 B 为什么笑了？

同学 B 笑是因为他就是小说的作者，室友并不知道。

Part 2 书面练习

选词填空 Choose a word to fill in each blank

1. 内容　2. 修改　3. 小说　4. 更新　5. 终于　6. 没想到

完成句子 Complete the sentences

1. 再坚持一会儿，我们已经爬到一半了，不能半途而废。
2. 我来中国已经 2 年了。
3. 我以为会下雨，没想到一直是大太阳。
4. 我减肥一年了，现在终于瘦下来了。

句子配对 Match the sentences

1.B　2.F　3.A　4.E　5.C　6.D

Part 3 拓展练习

复述课文 Repeat the text

同学 A 推开门走进宿舍，这时同学 B 在网上写小说。

同学 A 坐下后兴奋地说："啊！终于更新了！"

同学 B 问："什么更新了？"

同学 A 回答："是我之前看的一部小说，已经很久没有出过新内容了。我以为作者已经半途而废了，没想到今天他又更新了。"

同学 B 说："哦……"，然后他笑了。

最后，同学 B 的电脑显示"发表成功"。

8 作业风波：“借鉴”
Assignment disturbance: use for reference

综合练习 COMPREHENSIVE PRACTICE

Part 1 视频练习

看视频，将句子和说话人的语气连线
Connect the following sentences with the speaker's tone

1.B 2.E 3.D 4.A 5.C

看视频，选择填空 Watch the video and choose the best answer

1.B 2.C 3.A 4.C

看视频，回答问题 Watch the video and answer the questions

1. 同学 B 认为同学 A 的作品怎么样？

同学 B 觉得一般，没什么特殊的。

2. 同学 A 最终是怎么样维护他的正当权益的？

同学 A 和同学 B 去找了刘老师，刘老师把同学 B 的成绩改为了 0 分。

Part 2 书面练习

选词填空 Choose a word to fill in each blank

1. 满足 2. 截止 3. 维护 4. 发表 5. 整理 6. 投稿

完成句子 Complete the sentences

1. 你想吃啥？
2. 道具很容易做。
3. 没想到今天的作业这么简单。
4. 我觉得很一般。
5. 周末我在家看看书、打扫打扫卫生。

句子配对 Match the sentences

1.C 2.F 3.A 4.B 5.D 6.E

Part 3 拓展练习

复述课文 Repeat the text

同学A边整理作品集边敲门。

同学B开门后问他："看啥呢？"同学A回答："我正在整理作品。"同学B说："这么多，你没少画吧。"同学A回答："还好还好，就这样吧。"同学B又说："你已经获了那么多奖了，你就满足吧！"

这时，同学A接到外卖员的电话，他说："喂，你好。好的，我现在就去拿。"

同学A走后，同学B去看了他的平板电脑，同学B边看边说："我记得密码是……也就一般吧，没什么特殊的。他怎么这么容易获奖呢？这张好像还不错。"然后他拿出手机拍下同学A的作品。

几天后，同学B发现截止日期是明天，他来不及了，于是他拿出手机画同学A的作品，他说："借鉴借鉴，不算抄袭。"

两天后，同学B的作业得了98分。同学A很生气地说："你抄袭了我的画！"同学B说："我……我那只是借鉴。"同学A问："借鉴了百分之九十？你这是侵犯了我的知识产权啊！我的这些作品是要发表的，你先投稿了我还怎么发表？"同学B道歉："对不起……"同学A说："我们去找刘老师，这件事我需要维护我的正当权益。"

最后，刘老师把同学B的分数改成了0分。

9 气象小主播的幕后工作 Weather anchor: behind the scenes

综合练习 COMPREHENSIVE PRACTICE

Part 1 视频练习

看视频，选择填空 Watch the video and choose the best answer

1.B 2.C 3.B 4.A

看视频，回答问题 Watch the video and answer the questions

1. 吴鹏飞今天怎么没课？

因为他九点要去拍摄"信大小主播"的节目。

2. 吴鹏飞最后出门带伞了吗？

（回答时应引导学生说明原因）带伞了，他的室友今天正好不出门，把伞借给吴鹏飞了。

3. "信大小主播"的工作是什么？

（引导学生归纳总结整个视频内容，结合实际梳理节目的整个幕后工作）"信大小主播"的工作室进行天气预报，为大家说天气。

Part 2 书面练习

选词填空 Choose a word to fill in each blank

1. 准备　2. 正好　3. 拍摄　4. 稿件　5. 主播

完成句子 Complete the sentences

1. 我要去图书馆。
2. 可能不能去游泳了。
3. 天气预报说周末会下雨。
4. 暑假到了，你怎么回家？

连词成句 Match the words into a sentence

1. 我忘掉了妹妹生日。
2. 他想买件衣服。
3. 你怎么回宿舍？
4. 迈克周末要参加聚会。/ 周末迈克要参加聚会。

Part 3 拓展练习

复述课文 Repeat the text

吴鹏飞今天没课，他准备要去拍摄"信大小主播"的节目。他的舍友说今天可能会下雨，让他记得带把伞 。可是吴鹏飞的伞昨天坏掉了。舍友今天正好不出门，所以吴鹏飞用了舍友的伞。到了拍摄地点后，吴鹏飞说稿件准备好了，可以开始拍摄了。今天的气象小主播是韦杰卓，由她为大家说天气。

10 创业生活：加班
Entrepreneurial life of overtime

综合练习 COMPREHENSIVE PRACTICE

Part 1 视频练习

将下列图片按顺序排列 Arrange the following pictures in order

图片顺序为：C–A–D–B

看视频，选择填空 Watch the video and choose the best answer

1.A　　2.C　　3.A　　4.B

看视频，回答问题 Watch the video and answer the questions

1. 丁总为什么要写策划？

因为丁总准备推广产品。

2. 看完了视频，你觉得加班的时候丁总和他的工作伙伴是什么样的心情？

（无标准答案，鼓励学生说出自己的真实感受即可）我觉得加班的时候丁总和他的工作伙伴是一起加油、努力奋斗的心情。

Part 2 书面练习

选词填空 Choose a word to fill in each blank

1. 加油　　2. 加班　　3. 创业　　4. 准备　　5. 策划

完成句子 Complete the sentences

1. 真巧啊，我也要去考试。
2. 没有，现在还没上课。
3. 你写完作业了吗？
4. 那你吃饭了吗？
5. 他正在睡觉，没听见。

连词成句 Match the words into a sentence

1. 我一下课就去医院。
2. 她吃完早餐就去上学。
3. 爸爸一回家就看电视。
4. 我考完试就请你吃饭。
5. 马丁一到北京就去故宫。

Part 3 拓展练习

复述课文 Repeat the text

晚上八点，同学 A 在和丁总打电话，丁总在写策划案。

同学 A 打完电话走进办公室，他发现丁总还在加班。丁总正在写策划案，准备推广他们的产品。

同学 A 问丁总吃饭了吗，丁总回答："还没呢，等我忙完就去吃。" 同学 A 说："好的，我也过来加班了。加油！" 丁总说："我们一起加油啊！"

11 走，一起去 Come on, let's go

综合练习 COMPREHENSIVE PRACTICE

Part 1 视频练习

看视频，将句子和说话人的语气连线 Connect the following sentences with the speaker's tone

1.B　2.C　3.D　4.E　5.A

看视频，选择填空 Watch the video and choose the best answer

1.C　2.A　3.B　4.C

看视频，回答问题 Watch the video and answer the questions

1. 视频中，同学 D 的态度经历了几次变化？为什么？

同学D一开始不太想去，因为他觉得今天太热了，而且宿舍离食堂很远，不想走过去。后来同学C说现在校内交通很方便，建议他坐车去，所以最后他决定坐车去。

2. 视频的最后，同学们一起出发去做什么？

同学们一起出发去食堂参加包饺子活动。

3. 看完视频，总结一下校园里有哪些交通工具，并补充你知道的其他交通工具。

滑板，自行车，共享单车，小公交……

Part 2 书面练习

选词填空 Choose a word to fill in each blank

1. 打算　2. 听说　3. 参加　4. 优惠；好主意　5. 离

完成句子 Complete the sentences

1. 你打算去做什么？
   我打算去旅游。
2. 杭州今天 42 ℃呢，西安的夏天相对来说很凉快了。
3. 飞机票好贵啊，要不我们坐火车去？
4. 算了吧，我们去选其他的课。
5. 如果不舒服的话，就回家休息吧。

句子配对 Match the sentences

1.C　2.E　3.D　4.A　5.B

Part 3 拓展练习

复述课文 Repeat the text

同学A：听说今天食堂有包饺子活动，你们想去参加吗？

同学B：好呀。

同学C：可以。

同学D：你们都去吗？我不太想去……

同学B：为什么呀？

同学D：今天太热了，而且我宿舍离食堂很远，我不想走过去，还是算了吧。

同学C：现在校内交通很方便，要不你坐车去？

同学A：对啊，如果你坐校园小公交的话，几分钟就到了。

同学D：好主意！那我也去。你们打算怎么过去？

同学B：食堂离我最近，我准备走过去。

同学A：我想骑共享单车去，我买了优惠卡，相对来说很便宜。

同学C：我要滑滑板过去。

同学D：那走吧，我们一起出发！

12 网购真方便
Online shopping is so convenient

综合练习 COMPREHENSIVE PRACTICE

Part 1 视频练习

看视频，判断对错 Watch the video and judge true or false

1.× 2.× 3.√ 4.× 5.× 6.×

看视频，选择填空 Watching video and choose the best answer

1.B 2.B 3.A 4.C

看视频，回答问题 Watch the video and answer the questions

1. 视频中，"双十一"是什么日子？和平时有什么不一样吗？

"双十一"是购物节，淘宝上有很多优惠活动。

2. 为什么快递站有那么多人？

因为大家都喜欢趁有优惠的时候买东西，而且现在网购那么方便，所以这两天的快递特别多。

Part 2 书面练习

选词填空 Choose a word to fill in each blank

1. 正好 2. 适合 3. 网购 4. 平时 5. 日常 6. 赶快

完成句子 Complete sentences

1. 赶快写，交作业的截止时间快到了。
2. 正好我有两张票，我们可以一起去。
3. 不，这辆蓝色的是安娜的。
我的是粉色的。
4. 趁最近放假，我们一起去听音乐会吧。
5. 这两套餐具，我觉得淡黄色的更好看一点 。

句子配对 Match the sentences

1.E 2.C 3.A 4.D 5.B

Part 3 拓展练习

复述课文 Repeat the text

（同学 A 和同学 B 在宿舍）

同学A：你在干什么？

同学B："双十一"购物节快到了，淘宝上有很多优惠活动，我在找要买的东西。

同学A：你提醒我了，我正好也想买几件新衣服。

……

同学A：你帮我选一选，这件衣服哪个颜色适合我？

同学B：我觉得黑色的很日常，白色的更百搭一点儿。

同学A：那我买这件白色的吧！

（两天后）

同学B：呀！我前天买的东西今天就到了，你的呢？

同学A：我的也是，好快啊！

同学B：我们一起去拿快递吧！

（同学 A 和同学 B 在快递站）

同学A：好多人啊，平时都没有这么多人。

同学B：是啊，因为大家都喜欢趁有优惠的时候买东西，而且现在网购那么方便，所以这两天的快递特别多。

同学A：对哦～那我们赶快去排队吧！

"十二五"职业教育国家规划教材
经全国职业教育教材审定委员会审定

水利工程测量

（第二版）

主　编　赵　红
副主编　张养安　李聚方　刘　勇

中国水利水电出版社
www.waterpub.com.cn

内 容 提 要

本教材共分三篇、十五个项目。第一篇基础篇，包括七个项目，主要介绍了测量的基本概念、基本知识和基本工作，以及测量仪器的使用方法、基本工作的作业方法；其中项目一绪论，主要介绍了测量的基本概念、基本工作和基本原则；项目二地形图的基本知识，主要介绍了地形图的基本概念和基本知识；项目三测量误差的基本知识，主要介绍了误差的概念及精度评定的方法；项目四至七介绍了测量工作（包括水准测量、角度测量、距离测量）的原理和方法，以及水准仪、经纬仪、全站仪的使用方法；第二篇地形图测绘，主要介绍了地形图测绘的作业流程、外业施测、数据处理及成图，其中项目八介绍了控制测量的作业方法，项目九介绍了地形图测绘的方法，项目十介绍了地形图应用；第三篇施工测量及变形监测包括项目十一至十五，介绍了测量在水利工程中的应用，包括施工测量的基本工作、大坝施工测量、隧洞施工测量、渠道测量和大坝变形观测等内容。

本教材可供水利工程、水利水电建筑工程、水信息、水文、工程地质、农林、环境工程等专业使用，也可供从事水利水电的专业技术人员参考。

图书在版编目（CIP）数据

水利工程测量 / 赵红主编. -- 2版. -- 北京 : 中国水利水电出版社, 2016.1(2024.7重印).
“十二五”职业教育国家规划教材
ISBN 978-7-5170-4045-3

Ⅰ. ①水… Ⅱ. ①赵… Ⅲ. ①水利工程测量一高等职业教育一教材 Ⅳ. ①TV221

中国版本图书馆CIP数据核字(2016)第019515号

书　　名	“十二五”职业教育国家规划教材 **水利工程测量**（第二版）
作　　者	主编　赵　红　副主编　张养安　李
出版发行	中国水利水电出版社 （北京市海淀区玉渊潭南路 1 号 D 网址：www. waterpub. com. cn E－mail：sales@mwr. gov. c 电话：（010）68545888（
经　　售	北京科水图书销售有限 电话：（010）68545 全国各地新华书店
排　　版	中国水利水
印　　刷	天津嘉恒
规　　格	184mm
版　　次	201
印　　数	
定　　价	**69.**

凡购买我社图书，如有

版